The Dachshund

D1292198

Vintage Dog Books
Home Farm
44 Evesham Road
Cookhill, Alcester
Warwickshire
B49 5lJ

www.vintagedogbooks.com

ISBN No. 978-1-4067-8776-4

British Library Cataloguing-in-publication Data
A catalogue record for this book is available
from the British Library.

Vintage Dog Books
Home Farm
44 Evesham Road
Cookhill, Alcester
Warwickshire
B49 5IJ

www.vintagedogbooks.com

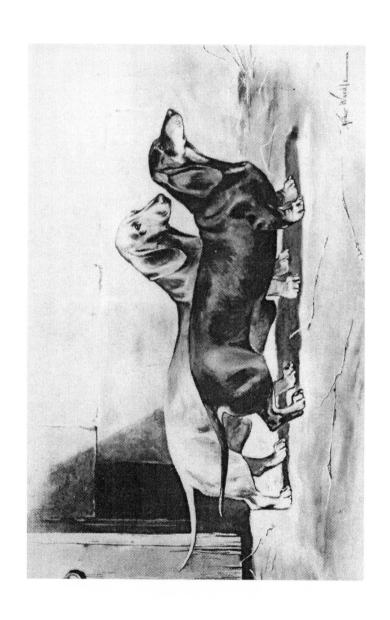

THE DACHSHUND.

WHETHER we shall ever get another dog from the Continent that, within so few years, has spread, multiplied, and become so much one of ourselves as the dachshund, is an open question. His disposition was genial, his habits were of the best, but he was quaint in look, and if not so autocratic in appearance as the Borzoi, he trotted behind his master or mistress, with all the airs that follow high life, conveying an impression that he alone had the right to be where he was. Then, again, he was not a fighting dog, and, though excellent as "a watch and guard," he was not ill-natured, and his skin was so soft and velvety that it became pleasanter to feel and stroke him than to do the same with a Dandie Dinmont terrier or another pet terrier that was said to be brought from the Isle of Skye; and he certainly appeared to be two animals rolled into one—a hound and a terrier—perhaps he is the connecting link between the two breeds.

With such qualifications he soon became a favourite, and from being represented in couples in the variety class at our dog shows he speedily appeared in scores, and had, as he has now, many separate divisions provided for him—challenge cups, and other valuable prizes, and a specialist club to look after his welfare to boot. These remarks, and subsequent ones, are in connection with the smooth-coated little hound as we acknowledge him, and do not include the rough-haired variety that has occasionally been seen here, and is pretty common in some parts of the German Empire.

Who was responsible for bringing the first dachshund to England I do not know, any more than I am acquainted with the particulars of the origin of the dog itself. Some sporting men of the old school have said he was nothing more than the common turnspit, which the cooks of their grandparents had used in their kitchens to turn the spit in which their joints and geese and turkeys were roasted. Perhaps there had been some connection between the two breeds ; there was a resemblance, for both had short crooked legs and unduly long bodies, but the cooks' dogs were seldom whole coloured, as is pretty nearly always the case with the dachshund, at least with our British variety.

No doubt either the dachshund himself, or a dog

very like him, perhaps it was the turnspit, was known in the East long before the Christian era. Old Egyptian and Assyrian sculptures, some of them 2000 B.C., depict a dog much after his stamp, but whether he was then used as a sporting dog or as a companion, or to assist in culinary operations, we are not told, all we know is that at the court of King Thothmes III. he was a favourite. Since that period he has undergone many modifications. Even within the past quarter of a century, since his association with our English dogs, his character has changed somewhat. In Germany, Belgium, and other parts of the Continent, from whence he came to us, he is used as a sporting dog, to draw or drive the fox and badger, but here he is for the most part used as a companion and for exhibition purposes, and his rapid growth to popularity is evidence of his excellence in both respects. Still, even our English dachshunds will do their work well when properly trained to the duty.

Comparatively few of our dachshunds have any chance of showing how good they are at sport. If properly entered they have no equals at their legitimate game of going to ground to fox and badger, when the latter have to be dug out. I do not for a moment suggest that he will bolt a hunted fox as quickly as a huntsman's terrier—that is not his.

game. All the dachshund professes to do is to find the fox or badger in his earth and remain there until you can dig to him. He makes no attempt to fight or attack the "varmint," but simply barks at it incessantly. Then if the game does turn his back upon his plucky little opponent, the latter immediately proceeds to business by a fierce attack in the rear, which is discontinued when the game turns again and faces the hound.

This description of work, of course, enables the hunters to dig with great accuracy in the direction the fox or badger lies, and the wary dachshund is rarely badly hurt, whereas the terrier that gets to close quarters with a badger, in his natural earth, will, as a rule, get terribly mauled. Still, I have had fox terriers that would bark and bark until the game budged, but this barking is not always good enough to drive a fox, and under no circumstances will it send either otter or badger into open. Particulars of a few day's sport with dachshunds appear at the end of this chapter.

When duly entered the dachshund makes an excellent line hunter, and Mr. Harry Jones, of Ipswich, tells me that his bitch Juliet was regularly hunted with a pack of Basset-hounds, and was about the most reliable of the lot. Of course, one has not to go further for an instance of the general gameness of the dachshund race than the trials with them on the Continent at both foxes and badger, which the best dogs have to treat much in the same manner as our terriers have to do here on certain occasions. It is quite the custom for such trials to be arranged at certain dog shows in Belgium and Germany for the delectation of English visitors, who, however, do not as a rule take particularly kindly to what some persons consider a high branch of sport.

About the period when the dachshund was gaining its popularity here, considerable correspondence about him took place in the *Field* as to what he was and what he was not, and, if I make no mistake, Mr. Barclay Hanbury, Mr. John Fisher (Cross Hill, Leeds), and others, gave their opinions on the subject. However, notwithstanding the complications likely to ensue on the introduction of a new breed, especially when one authority quoted Dr. Fitzinger, who said there were twelve varieties of the dachshund—a statement fortunately qualified by the remark that they were mostly cross-bred—all went well. In due course something like the correct article was fixed upon, and from that we have our dogs of the present time. As a fact I see less discrepancy in the type of the modern dachshund than is to be noticed in some other purely English breeds—the fox terrier, to wit.

Although some of our best dogs are accepted by German authorities as excellent specimens, still our British breeders have in a degree struck out a line of their own, and where, on the Continent at any rate, two varieties were acknowledged, the hound type and the terrier type, here a happy medium has been struck, and the handsome dog now seen on our show benches is the result. I have a large amount of information as to the work and general description of the quaint little dog as he is seen in Germany, and where he divides national favouritism with the Great Dane, but I fancy, in a book dealing with British dogs alone (and those that we have made such by fancy or manipulation) it will be best not to trespass on foreign ground. The Germans especially do well by their favourite dog, and the Dachshund Stud Book published by them is certainly, for completeness and tasteful elaboration, ahead of anything we publish in this country. As an instance of what is done in this particular, it may be mentioned that where the dog alluded to is red in colour, particulars of him are printed in red ink, and where he is black and tan the usual black ink is used. The same arrangement applies to the portraits of dogs, with which the pages of this Stud Book are thickly interspersed.

Some twenty years ago Herr Beckmann, one of

The Dachshund.

the German authorities, dealing with the different types of the breed, wrote as follows:

Having concentrated all varieties of the badger dog to one single class—the crook-legged, short-haired dog, with head neither hound nor terrier like, weight from 18lb. to 20lb., colour black-tan and its variations—we shall still meet many varying forms. With some attention we shall soon distinguish the *common* breed and the *well* or *high-bred* dachshund. The first is a stout, strong-boned, muscularly built dog, with large head and strong teeth; the back not much arched, sometimes even straight; tail long and heavy; forelegs strong and regularly formed; the head and tail often appear to be too large in the dog; the hair is rather coarse, thick-set, short, and wiry, lengthened at the underside of the tail, without forming a brush or feather, and covering a good deal of the belly. These dogs are good workmen, and are less affected by weather than high-bred ones; but they are very apt to exceed 18lb. and even 20lb. weight, and soon get fat if not worked frequently. From this common breed originates the well and high-bred dog, which may at any time be produced again from it by careful selection and inbreeding without any cross. The *well* and *high-bred* dog is smaller in size, finer in bone, more elegantly built, and seldom exceeds 16lb. to 17lb. weight; the thin, slight tapering tail is only of medium length; the hair is very short, glossy like silk, but not soft; the under part of the body is very thin haired, rendering these nervous and high spirited dogs rather sensitive to wet ground and rain. These two breeds are seldom met with in their purity, the vast majority of dachshunds in Germany ranging between the two, and differing in shape very much, as they are more or less well-bred or neglected. In this third large group we still meet with many good and useful dogs, but also all those aberrant forms, with pig snouts and short under jaws, apple-headed skulls, deep set or staring eyes, short necks, wheel backs, ring tails, fore-legs joining at the knees, and long hind legs bent too much in the stifles and hocks.

That we have not the latter in this country can with truth be stated, and I think the majority of the best dogs with us now will quite equal the standard of the best as laid down by Germany's great authority.

So far as my judgment goes, English breeders like Mr. W. Arkwright, Mr. M. Wootten, Mr. A. W. Byron, Mr. H. Jones, Mr. A. O. Mudie, Mr. H. A. Walker, Captain and Mrs. Barry, and others, have produced dachshunds quite equal to any that have appeared of late years at the leading Continental exhibitions, although, naturally, more specimens are bred there than with us.

I have been favoured with the following critical summary and history of most of the best dogs that have appeared in the show ring in this country, and, being compiled by one of our most earnest admirers of the breed, Mr. Harry Jones, no further guarantee of its value need be given. He says:

The first dachshunds that are recorded as winning prizes in England were Mr. H. Corbet's Carl and Grete; when at Birmingham in 1866, they were each awarded a prize in the " Extra class for any known breed of sporting dogs." And in these " extra " classes, all dachshunds had to compete until the show held at the Crystal Palace in June, 1873, when, for the first time, a class was given for the breed, and the winners on this occasion were Mr. Hodge's Erdmann, 1st; Rev. G. F. Lovell's Satan, 2nd; and Hon. Gerald Lascelles' Schnaps, 3rd; but from 1866 to 1873, dachshunds, whenever exhibited, were invariably winners in these "extra" classes, the chief winners being Mr. Fisher's Feldmann, Mr. Seton's Dachs, Rev. G. F. Lovell's Satan and Mouse, and the Earl of Onslow's Waldmann. Birmingham gave a separate class in 1873, the winners being Mr. Fisher's Feldmann 1st, and the Hon. Gerald Lascelles' Schnaps 2nd; this was a good class of fifteen entries, and they were judged by the late Mr. Lort.

At the Kennel Club Show, held at the Crystal Palace in June, 1874, two classes were given, "Red" and "Other than red," and separate divisions were given during the year at Pomona Gardens, Manchester, at Nottingham, and at Belle Vue Gardens, Manchester; whilst at Birmingham two classes were given, "Red" and "other than Red," when Mr. Bass's Slap was 1st, and Rev. G. F. Lovell's Mouse 2nd in reds, and Mr. Hodge's Erdmann 1st, and Hon. Miss E. Strutt's Thekla 2nd in the other than red class.

At the Kennel Club Show at the Crystal Palace in June, 1875, Prince Albert Solms judged the dachshunds and the classes were divided into "Black and tan" and "Other than black and tan," and there were thirty entries in the two. In the first named class H.R.H. the Prince of Wales won first with Deurstich, a dog five years old, bred at Sandringham, and the dam of Marguerite, the second prize winner, was bred by Her Majesty the Queen. In the second class, the Duke of Hamilton won with Badger, a nice red puppy eleven months old, bred by himself, and the Rev. G. F. Lovell was second with Pixie, a red bitch imported from Hanover. Pixie was very houndy in head, compared with the dachshunds then being shown, was smaller in size, with a beautiful arched loin. At Nottingham Mr. Hutton's Festus won first and also first at Birmingham, when he beat Slap, the 1874 winner. Festus won a large number of prizes, he was a very good bodied dog, but was short in ear.

In 1876, more dachshunds were exhibited with the decidedly pronounced hound type of head than had been previously shown; these included Xaverl, a most beautiful stamp of dachshund, full of quality, particularly good in loin, imported from the Royal Kennels, near Stuttgart. Most of our best dachshunds go back to Xaverl, and many of them are in-bred to him. Xaverl first appeared at the Kennel Club Show at the Crystal Palace in June, when he was placed second, Pixie being first; but this decision was reversed at Brighton. Zieten came out with Xaverl, and was awarded an extra prize, he was said to be the sire of Xaverl, though they were quite different in type ; and most of Zieten's stock born in England had his square, lippy type of head, short cloddy body, with immense bone ; whereas Xaverl was a most graceful dog, with beautiful neck and shoulders, magnificent loin, but light in bone.

At Maidstone, Dina came out and was awarded an extra first, she had a lovely head, narrow and straight, with a beautiful skull, good skin and bone, but moved badly behind. Fritz also came out at Maidstone, he had particularly long ears, was rather large, but plain in head, he was not so low, nor with so much bone as Dina. At Darlington Festus beat Xaverl, and again at Birmingham, but the judging of dachshunds at this time was very inconsistent.

At Brighton, in October, Dessauer, Chenda, Linda, and Schlupferle were new faces. Dessauer won first in black and tan dogs, and five prizes were awarded in black and tan bitches, viz., Marguerite 1st, Chenda 2nd, Linda 3rd, Dina 4th, and Frou Frou 5th. In the other than black and tan, Xaverl 1st, Pixie 2nd, Schlupferle 3rd, and Gisella 4th ; the latter was a very small bitch, light in bone and toyish in head. Dessauer had a long punishing terrier-like head, was too large, but very sound ; Chenda was houndy, but, like her dam Waldine, lacking in quality ; Linda was still larger, with a particularly long head, but flat in skull ; Schlupferle was a large red bitch, with a good head, but wanting in length of ear, and short of quality. At Birmingham, 1876, Major Cooper's Waldmann, bred by Count Münster, came out, and only obtained h.c., but in the following year, 1877, he won first each time shown, viz., at the Kennel Club Shows at the Agricultural Hall and Alexandra Palace, and at Birmingham, whilst at the Alexandra Palace the following year, when shown in excellent condition, he did not obtain even a card, such was the in-and-out judging of dachshunds about this time.

.In 1877 the dachshund classes at the Kennel Club shows were divided by weight as well as by colour, and few fresh faces appeared in the prize lists. In the class for "over 20lb." Olga, a nice red bitch, was first at the Agricultural Hall, with Dina second. Olga had won first at Bath the month previous : she was a houndy bitch, too large, and not sound in front. Her blood is to be found in a very large number of our best dachshunds, chiefly through Wag, her son by Bodo ; she also to Fritz bred that good bitch Flink. In 1878 another change was made in the division of the classes at the Kennel Club shows, this time by colour and height. A large number of dachshunds came out in 1878 that are to be found in the pedigrees of most of the dachshunds of the present day, and others only distinguished themselves on the show bench. These include Mrs. Hoare's Faust, Mr. Arkwright's Hans, Otto, and Senta, Mr. Hutton's Haufmann, Mr. C. Goas's Teck, Captain Shaw's Von, Mr. Wootten's Zigzag and Zanah, and Mr. Byron's Beckah—these were all bred in England, except Haufmann and Teck. Faust came out a seven months old puppy at the Kennel Club winter show, when he was second to his sire Dessauer. Faust won a large number of prizes, and his stock, more especially from Zulette, were very successful on the show bench. Hans became famous chiefly through his daughter Hagar from Linda, although he sired several nice dachshunds from other bitches. Mr. E. Hutton's Haufmann was a good coloured black and tan, another son of Dessauer, but better in head ; though too large, he was a celebrated prize winner. He came out in a dachshund class at Blaydon-on-Tyne, when he was placed equal with Xaverl, and at Birmingham he commenced the somewhat extraordinary performance of winning first for six consecutive years, viz., 1878 to 1883 ; still, very few of the present prize winners go back to him in their pedigree. Otto came out as a ten months old puppy, and won at the Kennel Club show at the Crystal Palace, beating his sire

Xaverl; he was a nice red puppy, but he lacked the quality of Xaverl, who turning the tables, beat him the same year at Bristol, at the Kennel Club show, and at the Alexandra Palace. At this show Zigzag and Senta made their first appearance, the former only getting third, but as he was but eight months' old, he had not let down and furnished, so appeared high on the leg ; still, the awards were very inconsistent as regards any type : Xaverl, first ; Von, second ; Zigzag, third ; Otto, v.h.c. ; Von Jostik (Zieten), v.h.c., and Teck, h.c. ; the latter had won first the previous week at Birmingham.· Von was much of the same type as his sire Zieten, cloddy in body, and lacking the beautiful outline of Xaverl.

Then Senta caused a flutter among dachshund breeders ; she had no difficulty in winning first in her class ; her skull and ears were wonderful, and her skin and bone extraordinary, but she lacked the grand outline of body of her sire Xaverl ; it was a great loss to the breed that she was never bred from ; Zanah, her litter sister, not at all good in head, became famous as the dam of a large number of winners. In 1879 champion classes were established, and Xaverl was the first winner at the Kennel Club show at the Alexandra Palace in July, 1879, beating Dessauer, old Erdmann arriving too late to compete; but his presence would have made no difference in the awards. At this show Otto was exhibited by Mr. Mudie, when he only obtained v.h.c. ; he should have made a valuable stud dog ; his sister Erdine bred a good dog in Mr. Parrot's Zänker, and also Mr. Southwell's Hannah.

Olympia, a puppy by Otto, came out in the puppy class in this year; she was scarcely six months old, and won first, the writer's Blitz being second ; Olympia was simply immense, much too large, coarse in head, but with wonderful ears, skin, and bone ; whereas Blitz was very small, with a lot of quality, and excellent loin. The awards at the Kennel Club show, held at Brighton, in November, upset all previous opinions of dachshund type, when Olympia was placed over Xaverl and Zigzag, the latter being again beaten by Zänker at Birmingham. The new faces in 1880 included Rev. G. F. Lovell's El Zingaro and Segesta, Mr. Byron's Jonah, Alma, and Hilda, Mr. Arkwright's Ozone and Octavia, Mr. Mudie's Flink, the writer's Jäger and Jezebel, and last, but by no means least in importance, Mr. Mudie's Thusnelda. Mr. Lovell's puppies were not sent to the Kennel Club show at the Crystal Palace, but came out at Stratford-on-Avon in October, where El Zingaro was second to the writer's Jäger, and in the bitch class Segesta was second to Octavia—a nice red bitch with capital loin, but not quite sound ; she was first exhibited by her breeder, Mr. Byron, at Chesterfield, when she obtained only v.h.c.; but she followed up her Stratford victory by winning for Mr. Arkwright first Bristol and first Alexandra Palace. Jonah and Alma came out at Chesterfield; the latter, a litter sister to Olympia, was spoiled by her bad carriage of ears.

Hilda, Flink, and Thusnelda all made a first appearance at the Kennel Club show at the Crystal Palace in June, the former, a sister to Jonah and Octavia, won in the puppy class. She had a beautiful type of head and ears, good loin, but had four white feet and a good sized patch of white on her throat and chest. Flink won first in red bitches, a good bitch with a coarse stern, like her sire, Fritz. The black and tan bitch class at this show was described by Mr. Arkwright, who judged them, as " a magnificent class;" and it is a question whether five black and tan bitches so good as Chenda, Beckah, Alma, Dina, and Thusnelda have ever competed together. Beckah came out at Oxford in June, 1878, when she was equal second with Zillah to Major Cooper's Waldmann. She had the much coveted arched loin. Thusnelda was considered by some breeders as being small and light in bone, but she was credited with having won first Hanover, first Munich, first Elms, and first Ulm. She was small by comparison with the others in the class, but dachshunds were undoubtedly being bred too large at this time, and an outcross of a small size of the hound type was very much required, and Thusnelda proved to be the very thing. By the end of the year she had gone from Mr. Mudie's kennel to Mr. Arkwright's, and the following spring she was put to Ozone, and bred the famous litter consisting of Maximus, Superbus, and Mignonne, from which so many of our very best dachshunds are descended.

Jezebel, a small Zigzag-Zanah bitch, with an excellent loin, capital body, but failing in head, came out and won first at Manchester when seven months old. She bred to Maximus, Joan of Arc, Joubert, Jocelyn,. Brownie, &c., all of which have bred winners. At Birmingham Mr. Wootten brought out Zadkiel, litter brother to Jezebel, but neither Zadkiel nor his sire Zigzag obtained even a card.

This inconsistent judging helped in some manner to bring about the formation of the Dachshund Club. On the day previous to the Kennel Club show at the Alexandra Palace in January, 1881, a meeting was held and the club formed, those present at the meeting being Mr. Arkwright, Rev. G. F. Lovell, Mr. Wootten, and the writer.

At the Kennel Club show Mr. Arkwright brought out Ozone, then seven months old, by Zigzag out of Zaidee (litter sister to Senta and Zanoh). Ozone was not entered in the open class, in which Mr. Wootten's Zadkiel won, but in a good puppy class of fifteen entries. Ozone was first and Zadkiel second, Zulette was h.c., and Jezebel c. In the competition for the cup for the best dachshund in the show, in which the following competed—Zigzag, Mr. Baker's Handsel, Alma, Octavia, and Ozone, the latter won.

During the various shows of 1881 a number of good dachshunds came out. At the Kennel Club show, at the Crystal Palace, Jude (litter brother to the famous Hagar) won first in the open class and second in puppies (a large class of twenty-five) to Hannah, a puppy of Mr. Southwell's, by Hans—Erdine (sister to Otto). Hannah had a good loin and nice type of head, but was deficient in bone. Jude, although possessing excellent type of head, with capital skin and bone, was too large and deficient in quality. At this show Ozone beat Senta for the cup for the best dachshund in the show.

Hagar came out at Chesterfield, bred by Mr. Byron and

exhibited by Mr. Wootten. She won first in the bitch class, and afterwards beat the writer's Jude for the special. Hagar was certainly a very beautiful dachshund, excellent in type of head, with capital skin and bone. She was on the big side, and not quite perfection in loin and stern. She has become celebrated in pedigree chiefly through her son Charkow and her daughter Rachel, that was bred to Graf III. Hagar carried all before her. At the Kennel Club show at the Alexandra Palace she beat Zigzag and Ozone for the best dachshund in the show. Mr. Benson's Rosa (litter sister to Hagar) first appeared at this show, when she was placed second to Olympia. Rosa had a nice clean, long head, with a capital jaw, good body, but carried her stern badly. The writer's Julian and Juliet, by Hans ex Dina, were prize winners here. In fact, no less than three first prizes, four second prizes, the medal, and the cup were won by dachshunds at this show that had Hans for their sire. And Hans was also exhibited, but he only obtained v.h.c. He was not exactly a show dog, but he proved himself a valuable stud dog. Juliet was nearly black with white fore feet, but she was houndy in type, had an excellent skull, with nicely set and low carriage of ears. At Birmingham, Mrs. Price's Neva (a sister to Wag) won in class for red bitches. She was long, with strong loin, and a very good type of head.

In 1882 the division of the classes by colour was abolished at Kennel Club shows. At the Alexandra Palace, in June, Mr. Arkwright brought out the famous litter—Maximus, Superbus, and Mignonne. Ozone, now shown by Mr. Walker, won in the champion class, beating Zänker and Faust. Maximus and Superbus were first and second in the dog class, and Mignonne 1st, and Zulette (now shown by Mrs. Hoare) 2nd, in the bitch class.

The cup for the best dachshund in the show was awarded to Mignonne. Of the brothers Maximus and Superbus—the former had more quality, was better in skull and loin, while Superbus had the better ears and more bone, and these qualities each dog seemed to transmit to his stock. Soon after this show Superbus went to Mr. Hoare's kennel, and, after the Kennel Club show, in January, 1883, Maximus went to Mr. Walker's kennel.

Grafin II. came out at Sheffield, and won in the puppy class, and afterwards many other prizes. She had a nice type of head, her ears were set on well, but were short; she was remarkably low, but her feet were long. The writer's Juventa, a long red bitch of the right type and a rare bred one by Zigzag ex Rubina, was second in the bitch puppy class. Mr. Southwell's Seidel, a puppy by Malt ex Erdine, was 1st, this was a nice quality bitch, but her ears were set on rather high and she was light in bone. Mr. Litt brought out Olympian in the puppy class at Cirencester, when he won 1st. He afterwards went to Birmingham, where he was only commended; but at the Kennel Club, the following month, he won 1st, Superbus only getting 3rd, being beaten by Faust III., a capital son of Faust and Zulette—capital body, legs and feet, but short in ears. Mr. Wootten brought out a puppy in Zeyn, by Zigzag ex Hagar—very good type with powerful loin, but not nice in colour. He won first in the puppy class and in the produce stakes. At the Kennel Club show in July, 1883, Mr. Arkwright's Lady made her *début*, and won first in the puppy class, the club sweepstakes, and the silver medal. She had a grand head, ears well carried and long, good body, excellent bone; her elbows were not quite right. Another good bitch that came out at this show was Mr. Byron's Sylvia, by Wag ex Beckah—very good head but light in body and bone.

Mrs. Hoare at this time had a strong team, including Superbus, Carlowitz, Vandunck, Gräfin II., Gretel IV., Rapunzel, Zither, and Zulette. Zither was most successful in the puppy classes. She was a very good dachshund, rather large, and wanting in loin. There was an excellent lot of dachshunds at the Kennel Club show in January, 1884. The four best dogs then going were in the challenge class, viz., Superbus, Maximus, Ozone, and Olympian, the latter won. He had a very good head and ears, but was beaten in body, legs, feet, and stern by each of the others. It was generally considered Maximus should have won. Mrs. Hoare brought out a chocolate coloured puppy in Drachen, bred by Mr. Wootten by Zigzag ex Hagar, a subsequent litter to Zeyn, when he won third open class, second puppy class, and third in the produce stakes. In the open bitch class some astonishment was caused when Mr. Askwith's Shotover was placed 1st and Mr. Hazlewood's Schlank 2nd, when such good dachshunds as Mr. Wootten's Zulima, Mrs. Hoare's Rapunzel, and Zither, and Lady (now owned by Mr. Knight Bruce) were in the class. Wiggle came out at this show, but was only h.c. She was a nice type of dachshund, but weakish in loin.

Warwick show was now becoming popular, and the dachshunds benched there in 1884 were a particularly good lot. Mr. Walker's entry at that show consisted of Ozone, Maximus, Hagar, Culoz (an imported dog), Zulima, and Zinnia—a team that could not at that time be beaten by any kennel. Culoz was only a fair dachshund, he being short in body and not typical in head. Mrs. P. Merrik Hoare had also a strong kennel of dachshunds at this time. The puppies by Faust ex Zulette were most successful on the bench, although several of them were not good in colour. Wagtail, exhibited by the writer, came out at Tunbridge Wells, when he won 1st. She was sister to Lady (subsequent litter) but much smaller, with a beautiful head, and ears set on very low. Wagtail distinguished herself by winning the prix d'honneur for the best dachshund of all classes two years—viz., 1885 and 1886—at the show of the Royal St. Hubert Society at Brussels; and still further distinguished herself by breeding the celebrated Jackdaw, who has generally been considered the most typical and best all-round dachshund we have had.

At the Kennel Club show at the Crystal Palace, in January, 1885, a very good lot of young dachshunds came out; these included Mr. Ingram's Sphinx and Isis, Mrs. P. M. Hoare's Kirsch, Edelweiss, and Graf III., the writer's Joubert and Joan of Arc. Joubert had previously won first at Cheltenham. The dog puppy class had twenty-seven entries, and the bitch class twenty-six, with fourteen entries in the third produce stakes; the winners in the stakes being Joan of Arc, 1st; Edelweiss, 2nd; Sphinx, 3rd; and Mr. Walker's Carlyle, 4th; Graff III. was remarkable for his beautiful skull and set on of ear, and these points he transmitted to his progeny to a great extent, notably to Stylograph and Jack o'Dandy. Joubert was a small dog, with very nice outline, deep chest, good loin, but was not particularly houndy in head. Joan of Arc much better in head, with a lot of quality, remarkable loin and chest; she continued to improve with age, and before the end of the year had worked her way up, and beaten her sire Maximus in the challenge class. Gil Blas came out at Warwick, but he showed himself badly in the ring; he was v.h.c. in the open class, and third in the puppy class. This dog let down and furnished well, and grew into a beautiful dachshund in body, legs, and feet, but was always a little faulty in head.

Mr. Arkwright brought out Belgian Waldmann at the summer show at the Crystal Palace; this dog had been very successful at the Continental shows before Mr. Arkwright purchased him from M. J. Gihoul, after having won 1st Vienna, 1st Spa, special prize at Aix-la-Chapelle, 1st and special Ostende, 1st and special Antwerp, and 1st Paris; he did not do much winning in England, but sired some good specimens, Belgian Herr being left to continue his line in future pedigrees.

The oddly-named sisters Decimus and Septimus were brought out by Mr. H. S. Dean at this show; the former was coarse in head, but Septimus, afterwards named Guinevere by Mr. Blackett, although not quite typical in head, had a beautiful body, with excellent loin and a nice size. In the puppy class she was placed second to Griselda, one of Mrs. Hoare's Faust—Zulette puppies, with wonderful head and ears, good skin and bone, but flat in loin; she eventually grew too big, and became unsound. Rubenstein was successful on the show bench, especially in the puppy classes, but he always looked like growing too big and becoming wide in skull. At Birmingham Mr. Ingram showed Indiana, a very good black and tan puppy, capital body, but a little short in ear, and in the same class Mr. Vale's Cerise II. was first shown, then a puppy under ten months, and a very smart dachshund she was, with good length of head, excellent body and loin ; she appeared a little short in ear and light in bone. Winks did some winning for Mr. Arkwright during the year; she was very typical, a good deal after the style of Wagtail, but not quite so long and low.

At the Kennel Club, Crystal Palace, February, 1886, Mr. Walker showed Charkow and Cusack, two houndy-headed puppies ; they carried all before them in the open and puppy classes, and were first and second in the fourth produce stakes ; these puppies were inclined to be large, but with excellent skin and bone, but failed in depth of chest and in the arched loin ; another brother (Cardinal York) was introduced later, and was successful on the show bench ; he was smaller and more compact.

At Warwick Mr. Arkwright won first, puppy class, and second, novice class, with Stylograph, by Graff III. ex Wiggle ; this grand headed bitch had been previously shown at Hanley, when she was second to Indiana; she had a beautiful skull and set on of ear, but was spoilt by a high carriage of stern. In May the Dachshund, Club and Basset-hound Club held a joint show at the Aquarium ; there was a good show of dachshunds—126 entries. At this show the writer's Joubert, after being second to Maximus in the challenge class, beating Superbus, and first in the reserve, came home with a cold, and died within a week. Mr. Wootten had some large classes to judge, but most of the winners had been seen before. Mr. Byron brought out Eve, a nice red bitch ; she won second in the puppy class, and was claimed by the writer, and winning five first prizes right away, when she caught distemper and died.

Belgian Waldmann's stock were brought out towards the end of the year. At Ipswich Brussels Sprout won first in the puppy class; she was a chocolate and tan, long in head, but a little high on the leg. At Birmingham Mr. Arkwright won first and medal with Belgian Herr, and Mr. Byron second, with Rufus, the latter being particularly smart, and of great promise, but unfortunately he died soon afterwards. Mr. Marshall did some winning during the year with Zenica, a smart young bitch with excellent body and loin. Jackdaw came out at Chelmsford in 1887, and quickly got to the very top of the tree, for at the Kennel Club Show at Barn Elms he won first open, first puppy, the fifth Produce Stakes, and afterwards beat the champion class winners Maximus and Lady for the Fifty Guinea Challenge Cup, and before the end of the year had won the title of " champion." Mr. Blackett brought out Jupiter at this show, and won second; he was a nice little dog, a great deal like his sire Joubert, with plenty of quality, grand loin, but just a little light in bone. Mrs. Hoare's Sieger was a particularly nice puppy, beautiful in skull and ears, but deficient in loin. He was successful in puppy classes. Jacobin, litter brother to Jackdaw, third at Hull and Birmingham for Mr. Mudie, has since won many prizes and done good service at the stud. Jocelyn, a good-headed red, with excellent loin, swept the boards at Ryde and Trowbridge; he is full brother of Joan of Arc, but not so correct in size.

Junker II., bred by Mrs. Hoare, and afterwards shown by Mr. Marshall, was a nice little dog, with excellent ears, and did a lot of winning. Herfrida, a very small black and tan, won a number of prizes for Mr. Mudie; she had a good body, the best of legs and feet, but became plain in head, which was never quite long enough. Mr. de Courcy Peele brought two nice black and tan bitches, Phryne III., and Phyllis IV., both good dachshunds; long in head, good skin and bone, and very sound, but a little short in ear; the former has bred several winners. Scarsdale Jungfrau, by Joubert ex Lady, was an excellent dachshund, of nice quality and type; she was 3rd at the Kennel Club Show to Guinevere and Wagtail, and won first the following year; there were few better bitches, if any, than Scarsdale Jungfrau at this time, and she ran Lady close for the cup.

Among the best dachshunds that came out in 1888 must be counted Mr. Arkwright's Julius, a dog probably wanting in size and bone, but with beautiful quality and type ; he was successful at Warwick, and at the Kennel Club Show, at Barn Elms. Pterodactyl came out at Birmingham, when he was placed third, he was then ten months old and not in very good condition, but was a sound active puppy, long in head, good in loin and stern ; this dog very much improved as he grew older, and furnished into one of the best of his time, winning the fifty guinea cup at Birmingham and Kennel Club Shows, and also won first prize at Spa, in 1891. Tinker, afterwards named Jack o' Dandy, came out at Liverpool and won first puppy class, and also the medal, a son of Graf III. and Rachel (litter sister to Charkow) ; his breeding was of the best, he had the beautiful skull of his sire, and is a great success at the stud. Mr. Ravenor's Windrush Rioter won at Birmingham, he had previously won at two local shows, and was an excellent type of dachshund, capital legs, feet, and body, but just a little heavy in head, which, however, did not improve with age. I have always understood that a sister to this dog, named Windrush Waldine, was an exceptionally good bitch, but she got hanged on the bench at a local show.

Mr. Byron brought out Duckmanton Harebell at the Kennel Club Show, Agricultural Hall, when she won first open, first novice, and sixth produce stakes, also a medal ; she had a beautiful type of head, long and clean. The writer's Jealousy and Jess Croft were both successful on the bench, the former excellent in head, with good skin and bone and sound, but carried her tail too gaily ; the latter was a smaller bitch with a lot of quality—her litter brother Jingle, never exhibited on account of an injury, was a most successful stud dog, and had one of the best heads since Senta's time. Mr. Vale's Melnotte II. and Venus II. did a lot of winning, and were two nice dachshunds.

Red Rose, bred by Rev. G. F. Lovell, came out at the People's Palace, she was a lengthy red bitch with nice quality. Scarsdale Julia was a small black and tan, inclined to be short in head. Stephanie won a number of prizes for Mr. Mudie ; she was an excellent type of dachshund but not sound. Several new faces appeared in 1889, but no particular dachshund of note, although some distinguished themselves as prize winners, these included Mr. Walker's Cito, Mr. Byron's Black Jack, Dr. Goullet's Jack Straw, the writer's Jay, Jam, and Jenny Wren, Mr. Arkwright's Switchback, Mr. N. D. Smith's Snapdragon, Solome, and Sheba, Mr. Mudie's Wolferl and Amsel, Captain Barry's Greta II., and Mr. Clift's Cawcawana.

Some excellent dachshunds were introduced during 1890, and, as several of these are now being exhibited, I will simply refer to their performances on the bench—Mr. Byron's Duckmanton Winkle, Mr. Vale's John o' Groat and Minimus II., Rev. G. F. Lovell's Chimes, and the writer's Janet, all being by Jingle; of these, Janet was the most successful, as she obtained the reserve to Jackdaw twice for the fifty guinea cup. A grand type of dachshund she was, she went to America in pup to Pterodactyl. Duckmanton Winkle should prove a valuable stud dog, he is the right size, of nice quality, and his breeding is of the best. The brothers John o' Groat and Minimus II., both excellent in head and ears, are somewhat deficient in chest and loin. Mr. Walker brought out Carl Rosa, and Mrs. Barry Jack Twopence and Reena, all of which did well on the bench, and are frequently now seen high up in the prize lists.

Some good puppies were introduced in 1891; several have been lost by distemper after brief show careers, these include Mr. Ravenor's Windrush Troubadour and Windrush Countess, and Mr. Woodiwiss's Keil, which were all very promising young dachshunds. Jack Boot, a brother to Keil, was a particularly smart young dog when shown in the novice class at the Kennel Club Show; and Mr. Mudie brought out a very good couple in Thorolf and Thorgerda. Mr. J. W. Taylor exhibited a black and tan bitch of excellent type in Hypatia, but she was too large.

The above contribution gives a complete history of the dachshund and the leading kennels in this country during the past twenty-five years.

The Dachshund.

Mr. Jones believes our modern dachshunds are far more typical than they have ever been, and with this opinion I thoroughly coincide. There may be cases in which legs, feet, chest, and loin have been neglected in trying to produce beautiful heads, but this has not been carried out to any great extent. The best dachshunds of to-day are particularly sound, have excellent chest and loins, and, considering their short legs and long bodies, get over the ground at almost an extraordinary rate.

Although, as I have previously stated, the dachshund is usually kept in this country as a companion and for show purposes, he is quite capable as a sporting dog. Personally, I have never seen one of the little hounds at work, so for information as to their abilities in this respect I cannot speak of my own knowledge. Again Mr. Jones kindly acceded to my wishes and furnishes the following very interesting account of three or four days badger hunting with dachshunds of his own. That they acquitted themselves with credit no one will deny, and at any rate performed their duties quite as well (perhaps better) as our terriers would have done under similar circumstances.

" I had some excellent sport with dachshunds in the spring of 1878. I arranged to pay three visits to friends, all of whom promised to introduce me to some badgers in their wild state. I started for Gloucestershire with two couples of dachshunds, each about three years old and well used to going to ground. The first time we went out was on the Wednesday before the Good Friday. It was full moon, and the night was very bright and still. In addition to the four dachshunds my friends ran four terriers. The earthstopper had gone on before and stopped all the main earths, and remained by them until we came. We did not net any of the places, our object being to run a badger to ground in a small earth and dig him out.

" From 2 a.m. to 5 p.m. the little pack hunted well, and were very merry sometimes; but it was the thickest underwood I was ever in. When you left a ride you were lost amid the tangle of brambles. A badger was viewed once, and had a sharp tussle with one of the terriers. The dachshunds kept well together, and on one occasion hunted out in the open for a long way, but I think they were then on the line of a fox. However, at about 5 a.m. it was found that one of the main earths had been unstopped, and two of the terriers could be heard hard at it in different places. Being well supplied with digging appliances we commenced operations, and about 10 a.m. had dug to one of the terriers, which we found terribly torn and bitten. After getting the terrier out, a dachshund was put in, and we soon saw him backing slowly out, and, to our astonishment, he brought with him a young badger, not quite half grown, dead and nearly cold. This the terrier must have killed early in the morning.

" The dachshund was sent to ground again, and he was soon heard baying close to where we had heard the other terrier, but his voice was so loud we could tell exactly where he was.

" Then, by about twelve o'clock, we had dug to the second terrier, and he was more injured than the first, so they were both sent home.

" The badger now seemed to shift his quarters, for, on putting a second dachshund in, we heard both dogs baying quite close together in a different place, and, after the quietness of the terriers, the loud baying of the dachshunds seemed to encourage the men in their digging, for there was no doubt as to the whereabouts of the dogs. About 3 p.m. we dug down to them, and soon bagged a very fine badger.

" Knowing, however, that there was more than one badger in, for the terriers had been working at different places, the four dachshunds were all sent underground together. They could not find the other badger, but one of them brought out another half grown one that had been killed by the terriers.

" I left that night (Thursday) for Monmouthshire, and after midnight on Good Friday we started off with the four little hounds and a couple of rough haired terriers for some very large woods, but with good rides in them. All the earths were well attended to with faggot bundles, the last of them was being stopped when we arrived. The night was cloudy and occasionally quite dark, but the dogs hunted very well, and were close on to a badger several times, but failed to mark one to ground. About 6 a.m. the dachshunds (both terriers had been badly bitten in the wood, and were sent to the inn) took a line towards the river Usk. This line they hunted very prettily for a long way, when two of them went to ground by the riverside in an earth about six feet below the top of the bank, and in a moment they were baying in a way that left no doubt they were at something. I was half afraid it might be a fox, but some hairs picked off the sides and top of the entrance proved it was used by badgers; and the unmistakable imprint of the badger's nails, quite fresh, close to the entrance, settled the question.

" Before commencing digging, the men expressed a great wish to send to the village for a noted terrier that was there; but this we would not permit, and they did not hesitate to say they had no confidence in a dachshund at a ' dig out,' but how they had reason to change their opinions will be told later on.

" The earth ran nearly straight under the field, not more than some five or six feet deep, and the loud voices of the dachshunds could very plainly be heard baiting their game. We cut a trench right across what we thought would be about the end of the earth, leaving plenty of room to work; but just as we broke into the earth the badger went 10 or 12 feet further underground, the dogs following him close up. Thus there was nothing for it but to dig another trench, having first securely stopped the earth towards the river. This second trench cut right into the end of the earth, and but for the spade touching the badger we should have bagged him then, but he went forward facing the dogs, and remained about half way between the two trenches.

" I then put the other two dogs in from the end of the earth, and at it they went, and whichever way the badger faced he was attacked in the rear.

" He showed himself several times at the mouth of the hole, but we missed him with the tongs. At last he made a bolt in a hurry, and over went the man with the tongs, who was then on his knees, looking down the hole, and, jumping up the corner of the trench, the badger made for the river bank.

"A shepherd had come to look on, and, having his sheepdog with him, the latter immediately gave chase, catching the badger up just as he reached the edge of the bank. The badger landed beautifully on the narrow ledge upon which the earth opened, but the poor sheepdog went right over the bank, down to the bed of the river, a fall of nearly twenty feet. The dachshunds were helped out of the trench, everyone ran and halloaed, and there was great excitement. The badger turned up a dry ditch full of brambles, and, by the combined aid of the dachshunds and the sheepdog, was ultimately bagged.

"On the Monday I was driven about fourteen miles for a third hunt, as my friend had seen a badger quite recently in the wood, and had made all arrangements for stopping the earths. I took the recently caught badger with me, as it was wanted to turn down, and the one we had bagged on the Thursday was of the wrong sex. The moon was late in rising, so we did not leave the house until 2.30 a.m. on Tuesday. The earth-stopper had all the main earths stopped, and a fire burning in front, by which he had made himself comfortable.

"This night we had only the four dachshunds;

they did a lot of hunting, several times running well, and giving plenty of music. They worked round the big wood twice, and when near the middle two badgers were seen quite close together, one following the other, and not far behind was old Waldmann, throwing his tongue freely on their line. My friend gave a view holloa that could be heard all up the hillside, and soon afterwards these two badgers were run to ground in a small earth. Waldmann got in before he could be taken up, and I could not get him out. I had particularly wanted to run a red bitch that had not done much work.

" We again dug a trench right across the line of the earth beyond where we judged the badgers to lie. To prevent them making a bolt we stopped the earth behind the dog with a large stone, leaving only a small hole to admit the air. We dug right on to the nose of one badger, which itself was digging as hard as it could, and had nearly buried himself, still we got it. Then we cleared the earth out, and in trying to get hold of the second with the tongs caused it to make a drive at poor old Waldmann, who was blocked in with the stone. The dog received an ugly bite, but we soon had our second badger in the sack.

" I returned that night with only one damaged dog, and three very successful ' dig-outs.'

" When we went to the stables for the dogs and Saturday's badger, and had not very much time for the train, we discovered our badger had got out of the box, and was not to be found. A cast round with the dogs and they marked him up the chimney in the harness room; he had reached a ledge in the flue, and get him down we could not, so had to leave him. He was ultimately taken and sent on, and I believe helped to make several good earths that are now used by foxes.

" The following moon I took the same four dachshunds into Warwickshire, where I had often been with my terriers on former occasions; but this was the first introduction of the dachshunds. We tried to run a badger into the nets, but were not successful, though the dachshunds found one in the meadows, and had some capital hunting before they lost him. There were a lot of rabbits about here, and I rather think they caused our hounds to run riot a little.

" After breakfast we had a walk round all the likely places where the badgers might have gone, taking a hardy-looking terrier with us, one, however, too big to get to ground. About 10 a.m. the dachshunds marked a badger in a nice little earth, and, before lunch, we had him in a sack; one man was bitten in the thumb by the badger, and our host was bitten in the leg by a dachshund. In the excitement of ' bagging ' he picked one of the dachshunds up by the tail, flinging him under his arm, and was stooping down and picking up another, when No. 1 pinned him in the calf of the leg. Needless to say he dropped the two dogs.

" The biting for that day was not yet over, for, when talking at lunch of taking the badger on the bank of the Usk, the question was raised, could the four dachshunds so hamper a badger in the open as to enable him to be taken with the tongs ? Nothing would satisfy the party but a trial, so the badger was turned out in a very hilly field, when he made off up hill, and from the way in which he bowled the dachshunds over, I have no doubt he would have got away, had not the big terrier been slipped. During the process of getting hold of the badger, a terrier puppy, about nine months, came up from the house, and hearing a great deal of ' loo loo,' and not knowing quite what to do, quietly seized the man who was energetically trying to get hold of the badger with the tongs, and left his mark on him.

" I have had many such days, of which the above are fair examples, and from these results am quite convinced that for digging out a fox or badger, nothing can beat a properly entered dachshund."

Although new breeds of dogs are being introduced, I fancy that the dachshund will continue to hold his own, for he is by no means difficult to rear from puppyhood, and, as I have already stated, is a desirable dog as a companion. He is, moreover, one of the canine favourites of Her Majesty the Queen at Windsor. Seldom used for his particular work in this country, nor for hunting in packs, for our beagles and harriers will do the latter better than he, and, in going to ground after fox or badger or otter we have our own terriers, which we cannot afford to lose; still, the dachshund has deservedly popularised himself, and when in his puppydom he has chased a sheep or made a raid on the poultry yard, it is no more than other young untrained dogs of our own have done and will do to the end.

The fact that the dachshund has a peculiarly nice skin makes him specially adaptable as an agreeable pet dog; and when to this is added a pleasant face, an endearing disposition, and, for a hound, a tolerable immunity from the aroma of the kennel, there is little wonder he has become popular. Perhaps at the present time his classes on the show bench do not fill quite as well as they did some half-dozen years ago, but this does not arise from any waning popularity as a companion and as a house dog.

What a dachshund in the flesh is like, Mr.

Wardle's drawings at the commencement of this chapter plainly tell, and the following standard, drawn up by the Club, will give additional knowledge to the searchers for information.

"*Head and skull.*—Long, level, and narrow; peak well developed; no stop; eyes intelligent, and somewhat small ; follow body in colour.

"*Ears.*—Long, broad, and soft; set on low and well back ; carried close to the head.

"*Jaw.*—Strong, level, and square to the muzzle; canines recurvent.

"*Chest*—Deep and narrow; breast bone prominent.

"*Legs and feet.*—Fore legs very short and strong in bone, well crooked, not standing over; elbows well clothed with muscle, neither in nor out; feet large, round, and strong, with thick pads and strong nails. Hind legs smaller in bone and higher, hind feet smaller. The dog must stand true, *i.e.*, equally on all parts of the foot.

"*Skin and coat.*—Skin thick, loose, supple, and in great quantity ; coat dense, short and strong.

"*Loin.*—Well arched, long and muscular.

"*Stern.*—Long and strong, flat at root, tapering to the tip; hair on under side coarse; carried low except when excited. Quarters very muscular.

"*Body.*—Length from back of head to root of

stern, two and a half times the height at shoulder.
Fore ribs well sprung, back ribs very short.

" *Colour.*—Any colour, nose to follow body colour;
much white objectionable.

" *Symmetry and quality.*—The dachshund should
be long, low and graceful, not cloddy.

Head and skull	12	Ears	6½
Jaw	5	Chest	7
Legs and feet	20	Skin and coat	13
Loin	8	Stern	5
Body	8½	Colour	4
Symmetry and quality	11		
	64½		35½

Grand Total **100.**

" The weight : Dogs about 21lb., bitches about
18lb.

" The Dachshund Club do not advocate point
judging, the figures are only used to show the comparative value of the features."

It will be noticed in the above Club description
that " any colour " is allowed, with only the proviso
that " much white is objectionable." The accepted
colours with us are red, black and tan, chocolate (or
brown), and chocolate and tan. There is some
variation in the shades of hue, especially amongst
the reds, some of which are so pale as to be almost
yellow. The black and tans and the deeper reds are

the handsomest, and a white foot or feet and a little white on the breast are no detriment. Mouse coloured specimens are occasionally met, sometimes with tan shadings, sometimes without. This is not a desirable colour, and "wall" or "china eyes" often accompany it. The dachshund is what may be termed a whole coloured dog, at least, this is what we have made him here since his adoption.

White as the ground colour is as objectionable in Germany as with us, but on the continent a greater variety of colour is allowed Herr Beckemann giving the legitimate colours, dividing them into four groups as follows :

"First, black, chocolate, light brown (red), hare pied, all with tan shadings. Secondly, the same colour without the tan markings. Thirdly, slate, mouse, silver grey, either whole coloured or with tan marks ; eyes, blueish or colourless (wall eyed) ; and fourthly, variegated, slate, mouse, silver grey with irregular black, chocolate or tan marks and blotches, with or without tan, and with one or two 'wall eyes.' Any one of these colours is as good as another in the Fatherland, but in case two dogs are of equal merit in other respects, the black and tan is to be preferred, or the dog most richly coloured and free from white."

As to the voice or cry of the dachshund. He is

not, as a rule, so free with his tongue as either the basset hound or beagle, but, of course, there are exceptions to this. One old hound, Mr. Harry Jones's Dina, was particularly musical in this respect, and her voice, in addition to being loud, was beautifully deep and mellow. Her daughter, Juliet, though equally free, had a much less pleasing note.

There is no doubt that where dachshunds have been entered to work with terriers and used for the duties usually ascribed to a terrier, they are inclined to hunt with less music than if used as a pack or worked in connection with bassethounds. Indeed, this is pretty much the case with all hounds, and I have known a foxhound hunt pretty nearly mute when alone, but in company with his pack be as free with his tongue as any other hound.

An instance occurs to me, that of Rally, a favourite otter hound bitch with the late Kendal pack. Bred by Mr. Coulter, one of the good old school of sportsmen, she had been entered almost singlehanded, and for a time, even on the strongest line, ran quite mute. After a season or two with the pack, she came to throw her tongue with the best of its members, and proved a most reliable and careful hound.

The Dachshund

HE dachshund is the only dog classified as a sporting dog by the American Kennel Club which is neither a hound nor a dog exclusively used with the gun. That it is used occasionally as a hound in the sense that it follows rabbits and hares by scent as does a beagle, does not alter the fact that it is essentially a dog that goes to earth and is therefore a terrier. Its name of badger dog is all the evidence needed on that point, and that it can be made use of as a beagle does not alter the fact that it is properly an earth dog, any more than the occasional use of fox terriers for rabbit coursing makes them whippets. They are now recognized as essentially a dog of Germany, although there can be no doubt that they were found throughout Western Europe at an early date. The description of the French dogs, given in the old French sporting books copied by early English writers as applying to English terriers, leaves no doubt as to the dachshund being then a dog known and used in France. It is very true that they were called bassets, but what we know as bassets could not have gone to earth, and the name was at that time merely indicative of their being low dogs, though it must be admitted that the name was also applied to the taller, rough dog. Apparently the French gave up the small, smooth, crooked-legged dog, and it remained for the Germans to continue his use and develop him into the teckel, or dachshund, whose peculiar formation has turned many a penny for the comic newspaper illustrator.

Notwithstanding the distinctly German origin of the modern dachshund, it is due to the English fanciers to state that they were the pioneers in giving the dog the distinction of a specialty club, for as early as 1881 there was a dachshund club in England, and that was not established until the breed had been recognised for eight years as entitled to individual classification. The Crystal Palace show of 1873, not Birmingham in 1872, as given by Mr. Marples in "Show dogs," was the first to give a class for the breed which, from 1866 up to that time, had been included in the class for foreign sporting dogs. Later, in 1873, Birmingham followed the Kennel Club lead and gave its first class for dachshunds. The meaning of the German word "hund" not being so well known as it should have been in England, led to the breed being given a class in the stud book of 1874, under the title of "Dachshunds (or German Badger Hounds)," in place of badger dogs, and this led to their being considered hounds and bred for hound heads in place of the correct terrier type. Indeed, it was not until the winter of 1883-84 that Mr. George Krehl, returning from a visit to Germany, took up the question of type and led the change to that of the German dog. We were in England in December and well recollect his talk on the subject and his saying that they had been all wrong in England, but he doubted whether it would be possible to affect the change which he intended advocating in *The Stockkeeper*, which he then edited.

Doubtless the dachshund had been brought to America in the early '70's, but we think the first systematic importation of the dog for use in the field was made by Dr. Twadell, of Philadelphia, who got them for rabbiting, and there was a good deal of discussion as to their merits as compared with the longer legged beagles. Dr. Downey, of Newmarket, Md., and Mr. Seitner, of Dayton, O., then took them up, and we have always been of the opinion that the "bench-legged beagles" of Delaware and Maryland had their origin in crosses with these early importations of beagles. There use as field dogs soon died out in favour of the beagle, and after that they must be regarded as show dogs, even admitting that they are favourite dogs with many Germans who go afield after rabbits with their Waldmans and Gretchens.

Whether it is that Dr. Motschenbacker, of New York, has such a very strong kennel that he has but one opponent of any consequence, we cannot say, but on his shoulders, and those of Mr. and Mrs. Kellar, has fallen the duty of upholding the breed, so far as the Eastern shows are concerned, and it is seldom that any other exhibitor gets in ahead of these exhibitors, who have done wonders in breeding and showing winners from their own kennels.

The one exception in the East is Mr. R. Murray Bohlen, who has kept dachshunds for a good many years and the puppies he recently showed at the Atlantic City exhibition proved that he had some good breeding material.

The dachshund is such an exaggeration that it is much easier to show

CHAMPION HOLLYBERRY
Property of Mr. Arthur Bradbury, New Brighton, Cheshire, England

DELVES LADY
Winner of thirty-three firsts and specials and two firsts in championship class.
Bred and owned by Mrs. Gerald Spencer, Lewes, England

CHAMPION WIRRAL HOLLYBRANCH
Property of Mr. Arthur Bradbury, New Brighton, Cheshire, Eng'and

The Dachshund

by reproductions of photographs what the best dogs look like, than to convey a clear impression to any person who has never seen one. His one distinct peculiarity is also that of the basset, the crooked forelegs, which is nothing but a deformity now scientifically bred. That this deformed foreleg is of any practical use in digging underground, we cannot believe. Perhaps we should say that its being better than the short, straight leg of the terriers which go to ground is not our opinion, and we put that idea away with the old-time belief that the loose dewclaw of the St. Bernard helped the dog to walk in, or on, the snow. At the present day, it appears from some recent remarks of Mr. Marples, that there is an attempt at doing away, in a great measure, with the dachshund front by English breeders. He writes as follows: "In these later days, there has been a tendency in England to moderate the crook of the dachshund . . . I cannot, however, go so far in the craze for sound fronts as to accept a straight-legged dachshund, as some judges do." In this, Mr. Marples is quite correct, for it is purely a fancy breed, and whether these fronts are deformities, or not, does not matter, usage and standards have made them properties of the dachshund, and it is just as easy to breed sound fronts as straight fronts; that is, legs that are properly crooked, so that the dog stands true on his feet and does not "run over," as a man does who fails to put his foot down squarely as he walks. We recognise it as a part of the breed, while we dissent from the claim that it is essentially useful in digging underground.

The German standard goes to great length in describing the dachshund, indulging in technicalities and minuteness of detail such as we find in no English standard. There seems also to be considerable difficulty in getting a good translation into language common to dog standards. The combination of a dog man who thoroughly understands German and has an equally good English education, does not seem to have been secured for the translation of this standard. The English long have had a short, clearly written standard, but it differs in several points from the German code, and, as the latter is the one in use here, that alone will be of service. We have seen three translations, and the one which seems clearest to the English reader is the one we give. It is better in its divisions into paragraphs, and clearer in its phraseology. The best part of the German standard is the illustrations, which show the ideal, and the faulty, conformation.

The Dog Book

General Appearance.—Dwarfed, short-legged, elongated, but stiff figure, muscular. Notwithstanding the short limbs and long body, neither appearing stunted, awkward, incapable of movement, nor yet lean and weasel-like; with pert, saucy pose of the head and intelligent expression.

Head.—Elongated, and, as seen from above and from the side, tapering toward the point of the nose, sharply outlined and finely modelled, particularly in profile.

Skull.—Neither too wide nor too narrow, only slightly arched, and running gradually without break (stop) (the less the break (stop) the better the type), into a well-defined and slightly arched nasal bone.

Eyes.—Medium sized, oval, set obliquely, clear and energetical expression. Except the silver colour of the grey and spotted dogs and the yellow eyes of the brown dogs, the colour is a transparent brown.

Nose.—Point and root long and slender, very finely formed.

Lips.—Tightly stretched, well covering the lower jaw, neither deep nor snipy, with corner of mouth slightly marked.

Jaws.—Capable of opening wide, extending to behind the eyes.

Teeth.—Well-developed, particularly the corner teeth; these latter fitting exactly. Incisors fitting each other, or the inner side of the upper incisors touching the outer side of the lower.

Ears.—Relatively well back, high, and well set on, with forward edge lying close to the cheeks; very broad and long, beautifully rounded (not narrow, pointed, or folded), very mobile, as in all intelligent dogs; when at attention, the back of the ear directed forward and upward.

Neck.—Sufficiently long, muscular, lean, no dewlap, slightly arched in the nape, running in graceful lines between the shoulders, usually carried high and forward.

Shoulders.—Long, broad, and set sloping, lying firmly on fully developed thorax; muscles hard and plastic.

Chest.—Corresponding with his work underground, muscular, compact; the region of chest and shoulders deep, long, and wide; breast bone, strong and so prominent as to show a hollow on each side.

Back.—In the case of sloping shoulders and hind quarters, short and firm; if steep (straight) shoulders and hind quarters, long and weak; line of

CHAMPION JANET

A prominent winner about 1890. Exhibited by Mr. E. A. Manice, Pittsfield, Mass.

CHAMPION PARSIFAL
Property of Mr. and Mrs. Karl A. Keller, Wellesley, Mass.

CH. YOUNG PHŒNOMEN, Jr.
Property of Dr. C. Motschenbacher, New York

CH. SMARTY WALDINE
Property of Mr. S. K. Gibson, Lowell, Mass.

HANNAH M.
Property of Dr. C. Motschenbacher, New York

HANSEL VON LICHTENSTEIN
German Champion—bred and owned by F. M. Widmann, Nuremberg. Mr. Muss Arnolt, to whom we are indebted for the loan of these photographs, thus describes Hansel: "He is the soundest, lowest and longest dog I know of. He has bone, true shoulders, perfect feet and a non-faddist head. Money has never been able to buy him."

The Dachshund

back behind shoulders only slightly sunk and only slightly arched near the loins.

Trunk.—Ribs full, oval, with ample width for heart and lungs, deep and hanging low between forelegs, well sprung out toward loins, loins short and tight and broad, line of belly moderately drawn up, and joined to hind quarters with loosely stretched skin.

Hind Quarters.—Rump round, full, broad, muscles hard and plastic; pelvis bone not too short, broad and strongly developed, set moderately sloping.

Fore Legs.—Upper arm of equal length with, and at right angles to, shoulders, strong-boned and well muscled, lying close to ribs, but moving freely up to shoulder blade. Lower arm short, as compared with other animals, slightly inclined inward; strongly muscled and plastic toward front and outside, inside and back parts stretched by hard tendons.

Hind Legs.—Thigh bone strong, of good length, and joined to pelvis at right angles; thighs strong and with hard muscles; buttocks well rounded out; knee joint developed in length; lower leg short in comparison with other animals, at right angles to thigh bone, and firmly muscled; ankle bones well apart, with strong, well-sprung heel and broad Achilles tendons.

Feet.—Fore feet broad and sloping outward; hind feet smaller and narrower; toes always close together, with distinct bend in each toe; nails strong and regularly pointed outward; thick soles.

Tail.—Set on at medium height and firmly; not too long, tapering without too great curvature, not carried too high, well (but not too much) haired. (A brush tail is, however, better than one without, or with too little, hair; for to breed a weather-proof coat must always be the aim.)

Coat.—Short, thick as possible, glossy, greasy (not harsh and dry), equally covering entire body (never showing bare spots).

Colour.—(a) Single-coloured: Red, yellowish-red, yellow or red or yellow with black points; but one colour only is preferable, and red is better than yellowish red, and yellow. White is also allowed. Nose and nails black, red also permitted, but not desirable.

(b) Two-coloured: Deep black, or brown, or grey, each with yellow or reddish brown spots over the eyes, on the sides of the jaws and lower lips, on the inner rim of ear, on the breast, on the inside and back of legs, under the tail, and from there down one third to one half of the under side of the tail.

Nose and nails black in black dogs, brown in brown dogs, grey in grey dogs, and also flesh colour.

In one and two-coloured dogs, white is permissible, but only to the smallest possible extent, as spot or small streaks on breast.

(c) Spotted: Ground is a shining silver grey, or even white with dark, irregular spots (large spots are undesirable), of dark grey, brown, yellowish red, or black.

Neither the light nor the dark colours should predominate. The main factor is such a general appearance that, at some distance, the dog shall show an indefinite and varied colour which renders him particularly useful as a hunting dog. The russet-brown marks are darker in darker-spotted dogs, and yellower in the lighter ones, and there may be an indication of these in the case of a white foundation. Light eyes are permitted; when the ground colour is white, a flesh-coloured or spotted nose is not a fault. White marks are not desirable in dark dogs, but are not to be regarded as faults which disqualify.

Height at Shoulder.—7½ to 8⅝ inches.

Weight.—Divided into three classes: Light-weight: Dog under 16½ lbs.; bitches under 15½ lbs. Medium-weight: Dogs from 16½ to 22 lbs.; bitches, 15½ to 22 lbs. Heavy-weight: Dogs and bitches over 22 lbs.

Defects.—Too weak or crippled, too high or too low on legs; skull too wide, too narrow, or too much arched; ears set on too high, too heavy, or too short; also set on too low and narrow, or long or slack; stop too pronounced and goggle-eyes; nasal bone too short or pressed in; lips too pointed or too deep; over-shot; short, developed neck; fore legs badly developed, twisted, or poorly muscled, hare-footed or flat-spread toes; too deeply sunk behind shoulders, i.e., hollow-backed; loins too much arched and weak; ribs too flat or too short; rump higher than shoulders; chest too short or too flat; loins arched like a greyhound; hind quarters too narrow and poor in muscle; cow-hocked; tail set on high, and carried too high or too much curled; too thin, long, or hairless (rat-tailed); coat too thick, too coarse, too fine, or too thin; colour dead, dull, or too much mixed. In black dogs with russet-brown marks (tan), these latter should not extend too far, particularly on the ears.

OUNDS form a very large section of the dog family, as the term embraces all dogs which follow game either by sight or by scent. Of the former section the leading member of the present time is the greyhound, and has as its consorts the Irish wolfhound, the Scottish deerhound and the Russian wolfhound. To these may be added the later-made breed for racing and rabbit coursing, called the whippet or snap dog. Of the hounds that follow the quarry by scent we have the bloodhound, foxhound, harrier, beagle and basset; and up to a short time ago there was another variety of large foxhound called the staghound or buckhound, which was used in deer hunting, such as the Royal hunt after carted deer, or after wild deer in some of the still remaining sections of England where they were to be found. The Royal buckhounds were given up some years ago and the carted-deer hunts having fallen into disrepute as had the annual cockney Epping Hunt. Staghounds are not a breed of to-day nor, indeed, are harriers to the extent they were. The harrier is the intermediate dog between the foxhound and the beagle and has been interbred at each end, so that we have foxhound-harriers and beagle-harriers; and the old type of true harrier is confined to a very few English hunts and is not in any sense an American breed, though some small foxhounds in Canada are called harriers or "American foxhounds" as the owner pleases.

Lieutenant-Colonel Hamilton Smith, whose researches into the origin of the dog and the individual breeds have never been properly recognised by modern writers, to whom his work seems to have been unknown, devoted much attention to the question of the early hounds. When he wrote regarding ancient dogs researches in Assyria had not progressed so far as they had in Egypt, and he was only aware of one representation of a long-eared dog, the others being erect-eared. He was therefore inclined to the opinion that the greyhound type was the older. Since his day, however, we have had the Layard researches and those of later times and the pendulous-eared dog was the prevailing one in Assyria, according to sculptures and tablets which have been discovered there. A large number of the Egyptian hunting dogs were also drop-eared and any priority which may be claimed as between the greyhound or tracking hound will have to be based upon some other ground than description of ears.

In old Egyptian and Assyrian representations of dogs we have to take into consideration the conventional type, which differed very much. All Assyrian dogs are stout, strong, muscular dogs of what we should call mastiff type. The Egyptian artists, on the other hand depicted their dogs as leggy, light of build and running more to the greyhound type, "weeds" we would be likely to call them. We know that Assyrian dogs were taken to Egypt as gifts and also as tribute, yet these tribute dogs are painted on Egyptian conventional lines, while the same type of dogs by an Assyrian sculptor are made altogether different. We must therefore discard all of them as truly representative, except where we come across radical differences between Egyptian dogs or between dogs of Assyria.

It was Colonel Hamilton Smith's opinion that, although Greek and Roman authors gave tribal names to some sixteen or seventeen hunting dogs there were but two distinct races: one of greyhounds and one of dogs that hunted by scent. One of these tribal names was the Elymaean, which name was claimed by some to have come down through many generations in one form or another till it became the limer, the bloodhound led in leash or liam to track the quarry to its lair or harbour. There seems also to have been a dog of greyhound type that had a similar name, but with an added "m," its mission being to race at the game and pin it by the nose, whereas the bloodhound was not used further than to locate the game and was never off the lead. In the Assyrian sculptures we find hunting dogs on the lead and they are also represented in a similar manner in Egyptian paintings, both erect- and drop-eared, or, as we would characterise them, greyhounds and scenting hounds. There is nothing in which custom is more of an heirloom than in sporting practice and the leading of the greyhounds in slips, taking the brace of setters on lead, or coupling the hounds, might possibly have had its origin a long way farther back than the Assyrian dog on the leash which Layard considered was one of the oldest tablets he had found at Nineveh. It is only about two hundred years since foxhounds were hunted in couples, and all through the old prints and illustrations hounds are shown in couples when led afield, one man taking each couple.

The Hound Family

There is no reason to question the statement that the hounds originated in the Far East and followed the western migration, or accompanied it along the Mediterranean to Spain and to Ireland, likewise across Europe, leaving the Russian wolfhound's ancestors a little farther west than they did those of the Persian greyhound; dropping the Molossian for Greeks to admire and taking more of the same breed as they spread over Europe, to give to Spain the alaunt and to Germany and Denmark the Great Dane. With them came also the tracking hound and the swift racing dog, developed by centuries of breeding for speed till it became what it is to-day: the perfection of lines with but one object in view.

In the very oldest Greek and Latin books, we find that fads of fancy then existed and certain colours were valued more than others, the highest esteemed being the fawn or red with black muzzle, the colour the late Robert Fulton always maintained was the true bulldog colour and known to us as the red smut, or the fallow smut, according to the shade.

Other colours referred to by Xenophon are white, blue, fawn, spotted or striped; and they ranked according to individual fancy, just as they did for many hundreds of years. It was not until about Markham's time that we find authors discrediting colour as a guide to excellence or defect.

How much original relationship existed between the smooth greyhound and the other racing dogs is something which has been taken for granted and not looked into very closely. The Persian and Russian are the same dog, undoubtedly. So also the Irish wolfhound and the Scottish deerhound, while the smooth greyhound differs from the others as they also differ between themselves. Because they are much alike in shape is not to our mind sufficient evidence upon which to say that they are the same dogs changed by climatic influences, as Buffon held. Buffon maintained that a dog taken to a cold country developed in one direction, while a similar dog sent to a warm climate produced something quite different. Size, conformation, and coat were all changed, according to that authority, and he gave the French matin credit for being the progenitor of a large number of breeds upon that supposition. Climate has influence beyond a doubt, but there are other things just as important, one of which is selection. As far back as men knew anything they must have known that the way to get fast dogs was to breed fast dogs together; and if in eight generations it is possible to completely breed out a bulldog cross on a greyhound, as we shall show later on was accomplished, what is to prevent men all over the world taking any

The Dog Book

kind of medium-sized dogs and breeding them into greyhounds in shape, and eventually approaching them in speed ? We have an instance to hand in the Irish wolfhound, which was extinct, yet by crossing Danes and deerhounds a dog of the required type was produced in a very few years. Whippets are the production of about thirty years of breeding between terriers of various breeds, crossed with Italian greyhounds and small greyhounds—and what is more symmetrical than a whippet of class?

The very name of greyhound is to our mind proof that this dog was originally a much smaller and very ordinary dog. Efforts have been made to prove that the greyhound was the most highly valued of all the dogs, hence and in keeping therewith a high origin was necessary for the word grey. According to some it was a derivation from Grew or Greek hound; Jesse held that "originally it was most likely grehund and meant the noble, great, or prize hound." Caius held that the origin of the word was "Gradus in latine, in Englishe degree. Because among all dogges these are the most principall, occupying the chiefest places and being absolutely the best of the gentle kinde of houndes." Mr. Baillie Grohman thinks the probable origin was grech or greg, the Celtic for dog, this having been the suggestion of Whitaker in his "History of Manchester." We can see but one solution of the name and that is from grey, a badger.

There was far more badger hunting than hare hunting when England was overrun with forests and uncultivated land, and a small dog for badgers would have earned his name as the badger hound or "grey" hound. Contemporaneous with this dog was the gazehound, which ran by sight, and, as terriers became a more pronounced breed and "grey" hounds found a more useful field of operations, the latter were improved in size and became classed with the gazehound as a sight hunter, eventually crowding out the older name of the coursing dog. That is our solution, and there is no wrenching a person's imagination with the supposition that Latin was the common language of Britain at the early period when this name was adopted.

We find a very similar substitution of name in the scenting hounds. The term harrier has for so long been associated with the sport of hare hunting that it is common belief that the dog got his name from the hare. A study of Caius would have caused some doubt as to that, for he only names the bloodhound and harrier as hounds of scent. The harrier was the universal hunting dog of his day, being used for the fox, hare, wolf, hart, buck, badger, otter, polecat, weasel, and rabbit. They were also used

The Hound Family

for the "lobster," a very old name for the stoat or martin; but this not being known to a French sporting author, he undertook to instruct his fellow countrymen how to catch rabbits by putting a crawfish into the burrows, having first netted all exits. The crawfish was supposed to crawl in till he got to the rabbits and then nip them till they made a bolt into one of the nets. If we did not have the French book with the instructions in we would feel inclined to doubt the truth of this story, to which, if we mistake not, we first saw reference in one of Colonel Thornton's books.

The meaning of harrier was originally to harry, to rouse the game, and had no reference to hares at all, it being more in regard to deer. In an Act of Parliament of one of the Georges this meaning is given to the name harrier, and was ridiculed in a sporting dictionary of about 1800. From the old spelling of the word, or the variety of methods of spelling it, there is ample evidence that the writers made no attempt to connect the dog with the hare. The Duke of York writes of "heirers," and other spellings are hayrers, hayreres, herettoir, heyrettars, herettor, hairetti. It will be noted that four of these spellings have "e" as the first vowel, while at that time the word hare was always spelt with an "a"; the spelling of harrier then began to change, and "a" replaced the "e" as the first vowel, and when harrier became thoroughly established the name eventually became more associated with the hounds specially kept for hare hunting until it was given to no other, and it finally became accepted that the harrier was a dog kept for hare hunting, and presumably always had been. That is something we can trace, but the probable transfer of the name of the badger dog to the hare courser is something that must have taken place years before writing was used to any extent in England.

The old name for running hounds in common use in Europe was brach in one of its many forms. Shakespeare uses the term several times, such as "I had rather hear Lady, my brach, howl in Irish." "Mastiff, greyhound, mongrel grim, hound or spaniel, brach or lym." Mr. Baillie Grohman gives the quotation from "Taming of the Shrew" as follows:—"Huntsman, I charge thee, tender well my hounds, brach Merriman—the poor cur is embossed," but it is now generally held that it should be "trash Merriman— the poor cur is embossed," otherwise, "take care of Merriman, the poor dog is tired out."

Nathaniel Cox, whose "Gentleman's Recreation" went through several editions from 1674 to 1721, gives "rache" as the latest rendering of the word.

The Dog Book

Cox is exceedingly unreliable as an authority, because he copied wholesale from old authors, with only a few alterations of his own. In the quotation referred to he says there were in England and Scotland but "two kinds of hunting dogs, and nowhere else in all the world." These are specified as the rache, with brache as feminine, and the sleuth hound. Here he differs from Caius who gives rache as the Scottish equivalent for the English brache.

Cox copied from some author the statement that the beagle was the gazehound, yet he describes the latter exactly as Caius did, stating that it ran entirely by sight and was "little beholden in hunting to its nose or smelling, but of sharpness of sight altogether, whereof it makes excellent sport with the fox and hare." That most assuredly does not fit the beagle yet a little further on he says, "After all these, the little beagle is attributed to our country; this is the hound which in Latin is called Canis Agaseus, or the Gaze-hound." This is not the agasseus which Oppian states was "Crooked, slender, rugged and full-eyed" and the further description of which fits the Highland terrier much better than the beagle, as we have already set forth in the chapter on the Skye terrier.

Cox credits the greyhound as an introduction from Gaul, but if such was the case they must have been greatly improved in size, or the dogs of the continent must have greatly deteriorated. Quite a number of illustrations of continental greyhounds are available to show the size of the levrier of France and Western Europe, and they all show dogs of the same relative size as those so well drawn in the painting by Teniers of his own kitchen. A hundred years later we have Buffon giving us the height at the withers of the levrier as 15 inches, which is just whippet size.

We have said nothing as to the bloodhound, which is another of those breeds about which there has been a good deal of romance. Originally the bloodhound was the dog lead on leash or liam, variously spelled, to locate the game. An example of the method is shown in the illustration facing page 284, the head and neck of the deer which is being tracked showing very plainly in the thicket close by. The dog having tracked the game to the wood was then taken in a circle around the wood to find whether exit had been made on the other side. If no trace was found the game was then said to be harboured and to this point the huntsmen and hounds repaired later for the hunt. These limers were selected from the regular pack, not on account of any particular breeding, but for their ability to track the slot of the deer, boar, or wolf. This use as slot trackers resulted in the name of

DEERHOUND
By Sir Edwin Landseer

FOXHOUND
By Charles Hancock

GREYHOUND
By A. Cooper

HARRIER
By A. Cooper

BLOODHOUND
By Charles Hancock

BEAGLE
By A. Cooper

TYPICAL HEADS
From the "Sportsman's Annual," 1836

The Hound Family

sleuth hounds being given to them on the Scottish border. Naturally, in the case of wounded animals breaking away and trace of them being lost, these good-nosed dogs found further employment in tracking the quarry by the blood trail, and here we have the bloodhound name. It was ability, not breeding, that caused a dog to be drafted as a limer or bloodhound, and we cannot show this more conclusively, perhaps, than by jumping to the "Sporting Tour" of Colonel Thornton in France in 1802. In describing wild boar hunting he says: "A huntsman sets his bloodhound upon the scent and follows him till he has reared the game." He purchased one of these hounds, which had been bred at Trois Fontaines and illustrated it in his book and it proves to be a basset. Here we have the name applied, as it always had been, to the use the dog was put to and not to the specific breed of the dog. Colonel Thornton, in speaking more particularly of this special dog, said that the breed name was *briquet*.

The prevalent opinion is that the bloodhound is a descendant from what has been called the St. Hubert hound, and in support of this contention the favourite piece of evidence is Sir Walter Scott's lines:

"Two dogs of black St. Hubert's breed,
Unmatched for courage, breath, and speed."

The legend is that in the sixth century, St. Hubert brought black hounds from the South of France to the Ardennes, and it is supposed that these hounds came from the East. It was also said that some white hounds were brought from Constantinople, by pilgrims who had visited Palestine, and on their return they offered these dogs at the shrine of St. Roch, the protecting saint from hydrophobia. These dogs were also called St. Hubert hounds and it is stated that the white dogs were the larger and more prized of the two. The Abbots of St. Hubert gave six hounds annually to the king and it was from these hounds that the best limers were said to be obtained.

If we are to accept later-day poetical descriptions as conclusive evidence, then the St. Hubert hounds were magnificent animals, with all the characteristics of the modern show bloodhound, and with a deep, resounding voice. Records are not made in that fanciful way and what evidence we have is to the effect that the St. Hubert was a heavy, low, short-legged dog, running almost mute and particularly slow in movements. In fact, we are very much of the opinion that the basset is the descendant of the St. Hubert breed. As evidence in that direction, we present an extract from that exceedingly scarce work, the "Sportsman's Annual" for 1839. Who the editor was we have not been able to ascertain, but it contains a dozen beautifully executed and coloured dogs' heads drawn specially for this number, seemingly the first of what was to be an annual, but which was only issued the one year. We reproduce a number of the heads of the hounds, by Landseer, Hancock, and Cooper; that of the harrier by the later being, in our opinion, the most beautifully executed head of any dog we have ever seen.

In the letterpress regarding the bloodhound we find the following extract credited to "a small quarto volume of fifteen pages, printed in 1611, and very scarce":

"The hounds which we call St. Hubert's hounds, are commonly all blacke, yet neuertheless, their race is so mingled in these days that we find them of all colours. These are the hounds which the Abbots of St. Hubert haue always kept, or some of their race or kind, in honour or remembrance of the saint, which was a hunter with S. Eustace. Whereupon we may conceiue that (by the Grace of God) all good huntsmen shall follow them into paradise. To returne unto my former purpose, this kind of dogges hath been dispersed through the countries of Henault, Lorayne, Flaunders, and Burgoyne. They are mighty of body, neuertheless their legges are low and short, likewise they are not swift, although they be very good of scent, hunting chaces which are farre stranggled, fearing neither water nor cold and doe more couet the chaces that smell, as foxes, bore, and like, than other, because they find themselues neither of swiftnes nor courage to hunt and kill the chaces that are lighter and swifter. The bloudhounds of this colour proue good, especially those that are cole-blacke, but I make no great account to breede on them or to keepe the kind, and yet I found a booke which a hunter did dedicate to a Prince of Lorayne, which seemed to loue hunting much, wherein was a blason which the same hunter gaue to his bloudhound, called Soullard, which was white, whereupon we may presume that some of the kind proue white sometimes, but they are not of the kind of the Greffiers, or Bouxes, which we haue at these days." The hound Soullyard was a white hound and was a son of a distinguished dog of the same name:

" My name came first from holy Hubert's race,
Soullyard, my sire, a hound of singular grace."

The Hound Family

The name of the author of the fifteen-page book is, unfortunately, not mentioned, but he was in error regarding the colour of the St. Huberts in the Royal kennels and that of the Greffiers, as he spells the name.

Another importation of hounds was made by St. Louis toward the middle of the thirteenth century, which are described as taller than the usual run of French hounds, and were faster and bolder than the St. Huberts. These were described as *gris de lievre*, which may be interpreted as a red roan. These hounds seem to have been extensively used as a cross on the low French hounds, but no importation seems to have had so much effect as that of the bracco, or bitch, brought from Italy by some scrivener or clerk in the employ of Louis XII. This Italian bitch was crossed with the white St. Huberts and her descendants were known as *chiens griffiers*. So much improvement did these dogs show that special kennels were built for them at St. Germains and they became the popular breed.

Specimens of all of these hounds undoubtedly went to England and we may also assume that English pilgrims and crusaders brought back dogs from the East as they did to France, the progeny of which were drafted as they showed adaptability or were most suited for the various branches of sport, but it is more than doubtful whether any hunting establishments in England approached the greater ones of France. The Duke of Burgundy had in his employ no less than 430 men to care for the dogs and attend to the nunts, hawking and fisheries. There was one grand huntsman, 24 attendant huntsmen, a clerk to the chief, 24 valets, 120 liverymen, 6 pages of the hounds, 6 pages of the greyhounds, 12 under pages, 6 superintendents of the kennels, 6 valets of limers, 6 of greyhounds, 12 of running hounds, 6 of spaniels, 6 of small dogs, 6 of English dogs (probably bulldogs), 6 of Artois dogs; 12 bakers of dogs' bread; 5 wolf hunters, 25 falconers, 1 net-setter for birds, 3 masters of hunting science, 120 liverymen to carry hawks, 12 valets fishermen and 6 trimmers of birds' feathers.

It will be seen, however, that only three varieties of hounds are named, and these were the lines of distinction set by Buffon, who named them levrier, chien courant and basset as the successors of what are named in the foregoing list as greyhounds, running hounds and limers. It is therefore to England we owe the perfection of the greyhound, the preservation of the deerhound, and the improvement and subdivision of the running hounds into foxhounds, harriers and beagles, together with the establishment of type in each variety.

WITH the exception of the modern Fox-terrier, it is doubtful if the institution of shows has done so much for any breed of dog as it has for the subject of this chapter. The quaint shape and peculiar appearance of the Dachshund rendered him from the first a conspicuous object on the bench, and no doubt greatly influenced many breeders to take up the breed. His admirers for the most part speak very highly of the Dachshund; but few breeds suffer oftener from the attacks of detractors, who affirm that the terms Dachshund and canine inutility are almost synonymous terms. For our own part, though we do not consider the Dachshund by any means to be the paragon of perfection which he is stated to be in some quarters, we willingly credit him with being a good useful working dog in his own country. Conversations which we have held on several occasions with German sportsmen have convinced us that this breed is largely used in the pursuit of wounded game, and his rather slow rate of progress makes a Dachshund more especially valuable, as it enables the sportsmen on foot to keep up with him with greater facility.

The name Dachshund conveys to many people the idea that this breed was produced for the purpose of destroying badgers only, and for no other object. As a matter of fact we believe that though many Dachshunds are " hard " enough to attack anything breathing, they are not as a rule so well adapted for such sanguinary employment as for the more peaceable and less painful task of tracking wounded animals, or beating coverts like an English Terrier. As a matter of fact, we know of an English gentleman, who prides himself upon the "hardness" of his dogs, who went in largely for Dachshunds. Six months' experience of the breed convinced him that they were unsuited for the work they were expected to go through in his kennels, and he finally abandoned them in favour of Bull and Wire-haired Terriers.

As will be seen from what appears below, there are at least two very distinct types of Dachshund; and the Rev. G. F. Lovell, of Oxford, who is admittedly an English authority on the breed, actually adds a third class to the number. The Toy class which he describes is, we really think, an objectionable ramification of the other two branches, for on the Continent we have seen toys of either type, and have always considered them weeds. The two chief distinctions are the *hound* and *terrier* type, both of which are fully alluded to below; but it is worthy of remark here that in this country, singular to relate, the former type is supported by the South Country school of breeders for the most part, whilst the Terrier stamp of dog finds admirers in the North.

Mr. John Fisher, of Carrshead Farm, is at the head of the northern Dachshund world, well seconded by Mr. Enoch Hutton, of Pudsey, near Leeds, who has kindly given us a detailed description of the points of the breed as they appear good in his eyes. In the South the Rev. G. F. Lovell reigns supreme, having for his lieutenant Mr. Everett Millais, of London, though the latter gentleman has devoted more of his affection to Bassets than Dachshunds, as will be seen in the succeeding chapter. We, therefore, consider ourselves especially fortunate in being able to give the opinions of three of these gentlemen; for though not unanimous in their estimates of the points, the views of each party are thoroughly sustained therein. We also propose introducing several engravings, mostly derived from foreign sources, descriptive of the breed, as, from its rapid progress in public estimation, we are of opinion that the Dachshund will soon be one of the most popular dogs in this country.

In the first place we will begin by quoting from the notes kindly supplied us by the Rev. G. F. Lovell, of St. Edmund's Hall, Oxford, who writes as follows:—

"Though the origin of the dog generally is lost in obscurity, yet the Dachshund can claim a very long pedigree; for a dog resembling it is found on the monument of Thothmes III., who reigned over Egypt more than 2,000 years B.C., and at whose court the inscriptions state he was a favourite; and a breed of similar appearance has been discovered by Dr. Haughton on early Assyrian sculptures. No doubt further research would bring to light other notices of the same kind, but these show that the abnormal shape of the fore-legs is not due to disease, as has been supposed by some who have not studied these dogs.

"This peculiarity is more commonly found than is generally imagined. Besides the Basset, both rough and smooth, and the Dachshund of France, it is apparent in an Indian breed, in the Swedish Beagle, in the Spaniel of Hungary and Transylvania, and almost certainly in the old English Bloodhound, though judges, setting Shakespeare at nought, are trying to get rid of it as a deformity.

"It has been asserted by a popular writer—'Snapshot'—that the Dachshund was not known in Germany until after the French Revolution, having been introduced by the French *émigrés*; but however this may be, most of our dogs of this breed have come from there, and it is the head-quarters of the race. Yet the Germans have in this, as in other cases, taken little pains to preserve the purity of the race, and mongrels abound among them.

"They may be divided into three varieties:—the Hound, the Terrier, and the Toy, though, of course, these are crossed with one another. The first of these is more generally recognised in the south of England, the second in the north. The third breed, which seems chiefly to come from Hanover and the adjacent countries, is distinguished by its snipy jaw, broad flat head, and small size. It has never found acceptance with judges, who prefer a dog that looks good for work.

"Dismissing this last, then, we find two distinct types, easily distinguished. The Terrier—which I shall pass over in few words, as I believe the hound-character to be the nearer to the original breed—is a hardy dog, with broad flat skull, short ears, often twisted, higher on the leg and shorter in body than the hound; his stern is also not so long as the other variety. The Dachshund proper, as it would seem from old engravings, was a hound in miniature; so he appears in Du Fouilloux for his Basset *à jambes torses* is clearly not the modern Basset, which has been developed from the ancient badger-digging dog of the sixteenth century (just as in Germany itself a large Dachshund is used as a tufter). No one would think of putting a modern Basset to dig out a badger or fox, so that either the badger or the Basset must have altered, and evidently the latter.

"I shall refrain in the following notes from criticising the opinions of others who have written, often very well, on their pet breed, but will merely give the conclusions which I have come to after having read everything I could find, having kept and bred these dogs for some years, and having taken notes of some hundreds of specimens.

"The head of the hound is long and narrow; the skull conical, with the protuberance strongly marked, though I have never seen it actually peaked as in the Bloodhound; no stop; the jaw long and very strong; the teeth long, the canines curved; the eyes of medium size and somewhat deeply set; ears long, fine, set on somewhat low, and farther back than in any other breed; the nose in a red dog should be flesh-coloured, but this is to be considered only when the competition is very close; the skin over the head not too tight, the forehead being wrinkled when the dog is excited; while the flews should be moderate in quantity, but not coarse.

DACHSHUNDS, FROM "LA VENERIE."

"The neck is neither so long as to give an appearance of weakness, nor so short as to be clumsy; there should be a certain amount of throatiness.

"The chest is broad and deep; the ribs well sprung, the back ribs being very short; the shoulders should be extremely muscular and very supple, the chest being let down between them; the loin is light and well arched; the muscles of the hind-quarters should have immense development.

"The fore-legs are very thick and muscular, bending in so that the knees nearly touch, and then again turning out, so that a line dropped from the outside of the shoulder will fall just outside the feet; the hind-legs are not so thick, and many good dogs are cow-hocked. They are much longer than the fore-legs. Almost all good Dachshunds either have dew-claws, or it will be found that they have been removed.

" The fore-feet are exceedingly thick and large, the sole being hard and horny; the stern is long, tapering gradually to the tip, it is rough underneath, and is carried straight with a downward curve near the end, but when the dog is excited gaily over the back; the coat must be short, fine, and as thick and close as possible; the skin very thick and extremely loose. The two original colours were the same as in the Bloodhound—red and black-and-tan—but from a long continuance of careless breeding they are found of all colours; but colour in the present state of the breed should count for very little if other points be all there. In height the Dachshund ought not to exceed 10 inches at the shoulder, and a dog of that height, and 40 or

DACHSHUNDS, FROM " LA VENERIE."

42 inches long, should weigh 20 lbs., the bitches being lighter than the dogs. At the same time many of our very best specimens are a little more than this both in size and weight. The prevailing faults in this breed are too great thickness of skull, combined with ears short and badly placed; the jaw is very weak—in fact, not one dog in ten has a good level mouth, while many have a lower jaw like an Italian Greyhound, and cannot crunch an ordinary chop-bone. Others get out at elbows from want of exercise or from weakness, while some have knees bent over, a great defect; the stern is often carried too high, or even over the back. There is one more hint which may be of service to exhibitors—Dachshunds are too often shown altogether out of condition: they require plenty of exercise and not too much to eat; their social qualities and their great intelligence make them pets in the house, but the points of the breed must be brought out by hard muscle, and it is impossible for a judge to give

points for a loin loaded with fat, or hind-quarters flabby from want of work. In character these dogs are very stubborn and headstrong, not standing the whip; from this cause, probably, arises the doubts which have been suggested as to their gameness, as, if corrected, they frequently lose temper and refuse to work, but when in sympathy with their master and once excited they will hesitate at nothing.

"I add the numerical value of the points of the Dachshund :—

Skull and eyes	15
Ears	10
Nose and muzzle	10
Body—throat, neck, shoulder, chest, loins, hind-quarters	25
Stern	10
Legs and feet	15
Colour	5
Skin and coat	10
	100

"As to the use of points there is something to be said. First, they enable any one who has a dog to form some idea as to its worth; and secondly, when a judge has settled most of the dogs in the ring, either as not worthy of notice, or though not, on account of some great defect, fit for the prize, yet good enough for a commended or highly commended, he finds often he has three or four, or it may be half a dozen, dogs left in; it is then most satisfactory to compare the points of each specimen numerically, not necessarily in writing, to arrive at a right decision."

Mr. Enoch Hutton takes a widely different view of the case, as will be seen from the following description, kindly forwarded by him :—

"Very much has been written in the public papers—notably *The Live Stock Journal*—about the Dachshund, but not much to the purpose. It seemed to me that many persons who possessed a specimen (however moderate) of this interesting breed, although they had never bred a single one of the race, must needs 'rush into print,' without being able to help themselves, and give to the world *their* notion as to what an orthodox Dachshund should be; and their particular dog was held up as the correct model, which they advised all breeders to copy and aim at reproducing. Nor did it stop here: several persons who never even *owned* a specimen tried their hand at laying down the law of perfection in points, for the use and direction of breeders and judges.

"There were some few articles of relevant and reliable matter, emanating from the pens of one or two foreign writers of some experience—a few grains of wheat in bushels of chaff— but most of the articles were more calculated to mislead than to enlighten the reader.

"One of the pioneers of Dachshund lore in England was Mr. John Fisher, who has had much experience as a breeder and as a judge. Mr. Fisher's unrivalled old dog Feldmann was also the pioneer of his race on the show-bench in this country, in the days when even the judges had to be educated and enlightened as to the breed and utility of such an animal. I have myself heard a judge of some repute in the canine show-ring give it as his opinion that old Feldmann was '*nothing but a bad-bred bandy-legged Beagle!*'

"Now as to what a real Dachshund should or should not be like. He should be a *hound* in all hound-like points, the peculiarities of the breed only excepted—*i. e.*, he must have a hound's head set on a very long body on very short legs, and the fore legs must be very crooked or bandy without being much out at elbows or knuckling over at the knees, the *extreme length* from the nose-end to point of stem *should be* about *four times the height at shoulder*, and the animal should be massive, or, as some of us would say, clumsy and cloddy in appearance; in short, a big dog in small compass. The head should resemble somewhat that of a Foxhound, but must not be of so decided a type as seen in the Bloodhound.

"My plan is to reproduce the breed in its purity, and endeavour to get the best and purest blood possible to that end, but I will be no party to 'painting the lily.' It is difficult even in Germany to find really excellent specimens of the Dachshund which can be purchased, for the really pure breeds are mostly still in the hands of the nobility, and they do not care to part with even a puppy, except, perhaps, as a present occasionally to a relative or friend in their own sphere of life, or, may-be, a common specimen now and then to an inferior in position.

"The breed kept so select is preserved in its purity mostly, but in this, as in other breeds, unless the animals are properly cared for and kept up, there is no certainty of reproducing the breed *pure*. But the chances are that without such care the produce will be *mongrels*, with many of the characteristics of the breed doubtless, but still not the real thing; and I aver that many, very many, of the Dachshunds which are imported into this country are not pure-bred. But yet with some people an *imported* animal *must* be correct and pure. Even where the pedigrees can be traced back for many generations without a single stain or cross on either side, it is impossible to breed *all* correct and good.

"For some time there has been a lot of noise respecting the style of *head* a Dachshund ought to have, some breeders making it appear that a "good head" makes a good dog, and with some judges who do not thoroughly understand the breed, a so-called "good head" has been an apology for the highest awards to otherwise badly-made dogs.

"According to the new modern fancy a 'good head' seems to mean a high-peaked skull and down face, with long ears, no matter how snipe-nosed and weak-jawed the animal may be, while the rest of his body may also be faulty—*i.e.*, it may be small and weak in bone, flat-ribbed, and short of muscle; and such a one is often allowed to rule the roast at our canine exhibitions.

"Now I wish to combat this erroneous idea, and as far as possible to write it down, if it may be; and to do so, though late in the field, I will give my notions, with the rules and points by which I have been guided in my experience.

"A good head is an indispensable point with me, but there must be other grand qualities that must not be overlooked in a Dachshund; but to describe the breed properly it will be necessary to take point by point *seriatim*, and I will take the *head* first, allotting to it 25 points out of a possible 100 for perfection.

"1. *Skull* (5 points) must be long and flat—*i.e.*, it should form a nearly straight line from the occipital bone to the nose point, and have very little stop; and I prefer a moderate width of skull behind the ears, as I find a broad-headed dog has more courage than a narrow conical skulled one: the occipital bone should be well developed.

"2. *Muzzle* (5 points) must be long and very strong, for the size of the dog; the length from the lower corner of the eye to the nose-end in a 20 lb. dog should be 3 inches to 3¼ inches. The muzzle should be squarely cut, and broad at nose; the under-jaw strong; flews should be fairly developed, so as to cover the lower jaw, and rather more. The nose in black-and-tan dogs must be black; in red dogs it is often brown or flesh-coloured, but I must own a weakness for a red dog with a black nose and eyelashes, which is attained only by crossing reds with black-and-tans.

3. *Mouth* (5 points).—The front teeth must be perfectly even, and fit as close as a vice, so that a hair could not be drawn through when closed. The fangs—one in upper and two in lower jaw on each side—must be strong, sharp, and recurved, and all must be free from canker and disease (this I make a primary consideration whenever I purchase a dog of any breed, as being in my opinion the greatest safeguard against danger from the bite of a dog). I never saw a fine-bred dog of this kind underhung; I have seen pig-jawed ones sometimes, but never kept one; and either fault would effectually disqualify an otherwise good animal.

4. *Eyes* (5 points).—These always partake of the principal colour of the coat; they must be large and lustrous, and deeply set, and in expression should be soft and intelligent; and I like them to show the haw slightly.

5. *Ears* (5 points) must be thin, soft as velvet, and long enough to reach the end of the nose, or within a half an inch of it. In red dogs the ears are generally a shade darker in colour than

FROM "ICONES ANIMALIUM."

the rest of the body. They should be set on low, and should hang rather squarely with the front edges close to the cheeks, and not rise at the roots except slightly when the animal is excited, or at 'attention.'

"6. *Neck* (5 points) must be long, thick, and strong, with plenty of loose skin, but entirely free from goître or enlargement of the glands of the throat.

"7. *Chest* (5 points) must be very deep and wide, the brisket strong, and its point well up to the gullet. When the dog is standing, the chest should be within three inches of the ground.

"8. *Shoulders* (5 points) must be strong and heavy, and loosely fixed to the body.

"9. *Fore-legs* (5 points) must be very short and remarkably strong in bone, and must bend inwards from elbow to ankle, so that the latter nearly touch each other, but they must not knuckle over in front.

"10. *Fore-feet* (5 points) must be very large, splayed outwards, and be furnished with large and strong black or dark-brown claws. In some specimens the claws are often worn short from walking; but if very strong this is no detriment.

"11. *Ribs* (5 points) must be well sprung or rounded up from shoulder to loin; a flatness or hollow behind the shoulders is a defect, as it shows the animal has not sufficient room for his lungs to act properly.

"12. *Loin* (5 points) must be long and muscular and slightly arched, so that it is perceptibly higher than either shoulders or quarters.

TERRIER TYPE OF DACHSHUNDS.

"13. *Hind-quarters, hind legs and feet* (5 points). Thighs must be short and muscular, the legs fine and upright below the hock; *i. e.*, must not be sickle-hocked; hind feet smaller than fore ones; and the hind-quarters must not be higher than the shoulder.

"14. *Stern* (5 points) should be 9 to 12 inches in length, according to size of dog; must be thick at base, and also thicker again a couple of inches from the base, and gradually taper to a point; carried with a curve upward, but not slewed. The under-side of stern should be flat, and the hair should be parted and feather each side thereof sightly. A dog with a broad flat stern as described is a great rarity, and is held in very high estimation in Germany, where it is termed an 'Otter-tail.'

"15. *Bone* (5 points) must be large, and angular at points, according to the size of the animal.

"16. *Muscle* (5 points) must be large, hard, and particularly well developed and defined throughout.

"17. *Skin* (10 points) must be thick, yet soft to the touch, and remarkably elastic. No other breed of dog possesses the same elasticity of skin; the animal can nearly turn round in it when seized, or at will he can contract it by muscular action so tightly to the body that it is difficult to get even a pinch of it.

"18. *Coat* (5 points) must be short, hard, and bright, but it varies much in hardness according to whether the animal is kept in a kennel or in a warm drawing-room.

"19. *Colour* (5 points). The colours may be—(1) self-colours, *i. e.*, any shade of fallow, red, or fawn—the former preferred. (2) Bi-colours, *i.e.*, black-and-tan, liver-and-tan, or brown-and-tawny, as commonly seen in the Bloodhound. (3) Parti-colours:—tortoiseshell, or blue-and-tan grizzle with black spots (this colour is often accompanied by an odd, broken, or wall-eye). Hound-pied are very rare; but though they are not difficult to obtain, they are certainly not desirable. The best colours are fallow-red, black-and-tan, and brown or liver-and-tan, which is often the result of crossing the red and black-and-tans. I prefer brightish colour in black-and-tan for show purposes, and of these I like those with red 'stockings,' in preference to those with heavily-pencilled toes, which I consider partake more of the character of the Manchester Terrier than of the hound proper. Black-and-white I have seen, and have had one very good black one; but I am not very deeply impressed with the beauty of either.

"Having given my scale of points in detail, it will be seen that I have allotted them collectively thus:—

Head	25
Neck and chest	10
Fore legs and feet	15
Ribs and loin	10
Hind-quarters and stern	10
Bone and muscle	10
Skin, coat, and colour	20
	100

"I prefer the *self* and *bi-colours* free from white in chest, throat, and toes, but in the best of all strains these blemishes will often appear; and for a small spot on the chest I would deduct only one point; but for white toes I would deduct two points for each foot so marked; and a dog with white feet or legs, or with a spot or blaze on the head or face I would disqualify for the show bench, except in the parti-coloured class, although for working purposes it is no detriment whatever.

"For exhibition purposes I am a great stickler for colour and marking, as I consider it should be one object of breeders to make all animals as presentable as possible to the uninitiated public.

"I have awarded no points for size, as in Dachshunds we find that they vary considerably, some small specimens being frequently met with.

"These small ones may be equally pure, as regards breeding, with the large ones, and are often found models of perfection, and are certainly most fitted for ladies' pets, for which purpose the breed is unequalled for cleanliness and affection: 20 lbs. I look upon as the standard weight for a dog and 17 lbs. for a bitch; a couple of pounds either way may be allowed, but no Dachshund should reach anything like 25 lbs. If so, I should look for some impurity of blood, except in very old dogs, which often attain very great weights; and I do not object to a bitch weighing 20 lbs., but I certainly incline to the smaller weights.

"The bitches are generally much lighter in bone throughout than dogs, but at the same time they possess more *quality* or beauty than dogs, as is general with the female portion of animal as well as human nature. The large dogs are best for outdoor work; and I fancy that out of a pack of Dachshunds I could pick the best workmen by their conformation only. As to their ability, being hounds they are naturally most fitted for hunting, and possess extraordinary scenting powers, and may be trained to hunt anything, from a deer to a mouse.

"They do not possess great speed, yet they can get over the ground a good deal faster than a man cares to run; and being slow, they are not so apt to overrun the scent, while they do not so easily tire, but will follow their chase for many hours without a break.

"In Germany they are used to hunt the deer, roe, foxes, and badger; but in the south of that empire, particularly in the Black Forest, though they use the Dachshund to track the quarry, yet when it is too strong for them to kill, the sportsmen either use the rifle or a much stronger and larger breed of dog—generally a Boarhound, or cross-bred dog—for the finish.

"In the country they are used on a small scale for hunting both alone and with Beagles. One gentleman I know often hunts fur with about six couple, and many times have I seen the staunch and true little hounds, when they come across a dry stone fence—which abound in West Yorkshire—and which had been taken by a hare, work round, seek the nearest gap, and pick up the scent on the other side, a ten or twelve miles run seeming good fun to them.

"In covert shooting they are equal to any Spaniel, and when it is very close and thick, are superior, owing to their large fore feet and powerfully built fore-quarters, though in briars their ears, head, and shoulders get severely scratched at times, and yet they seem to enjoy it thoroughly, and never flinch on that account.

"They can be broken to quarter their ground and work the game to the gun, if it be possible, and may also be taught to retrieve.

"In temper they are somewhat stubborn, and require great patience in breaking, but when once trained their great intelligence leaves nothing to be desired by the sportsman who admires the breed.

"In hunting they give mouth, but may not be so musical as the Foxhound and its congeners; but this I prefer in covert shooting, as I then know the whereabouts of the dogs.

GROUP OF DACHSHUNDS.

The large paws and strong crooked fore legs are admirably adapted for working underground, while the length of head and neck combined enable the dog effectually to protect his feet when the quarry is reached, be he badger or fox; and put a Dachshund to either he will give a good account of himself. I write of the working Dachshund.

"There are some specimens of the breed which have never been educated, or that have been kept merely as pets, which would not look at a mouse even, but are for all sporting purposes quite useless.

"The dog I mean, properly bred and trained, is capable of affording sport *ad libitum*, whether in the open or in the covert. For courage or pluck I will back them against any breed.

"Cats they do not stand on any ceremony with, and I will give an instance. Some time ago we were fearfully overrun with cats, some of which came from great distances after the chickens, and often carried off full-grown bantam fowls; and one summer afternoon my little bitch Vixen hunted a very large Tom to bay in a stone quarry in my grounds. The hole or fissure in the rock was scarcely large enough for a cat to turn in, and was about three yards to the far end, and sloping upwards. Such a customer in such a corner was not easy to dislodge, and not caring to risk Vixen's eyes at such terrible odds, I caught her, and sent for my black-and-tan brood bitch Maud, 18 lbs. weight, and turned her in. There was not much noise, but in a few seconds the bitch backed out, bringing the cat firmly gripped by the brisket, while the cat's claws and teeth were as firmly embedded in her head and face, which I fully expected to see well ripped up by his hind claws; but both rolled down to the bottom of the quarry, the cat quite dead, and the bitch none the worse save a few gashes on her head, the whole taking far less time than it does to relate it.

"To give another instance of their power of jaw. I have had a little bitch only 15 lbs. weight turn a hedgehog out of a drain, and grip the prickly ball heedless of the spikes, and crush it with as much ease seemingly as a Terrier does a rat, and make no bones, or rather leave no bones whole, about it; and I have never seen even a pup of a few months old attempt to open the soft parts out before commencing the work of destruction. Young ones will worry at a hedgehog, pull it about, and make a great noise; but a staunch dog, though he may grumble a bit at the spikes, does not mind them; nor when the affair is over is there any bleeding at the mouth, unless some of the points penetrate between the gum and the teeth.

"For memory they are second to no other breed; for an affront they take a lot of coaxing to gain their friendship—(two years ago my bitch Puzzle was troubled with rheumatics, and I applied a stimulating liniment; and for a whole twelve months afterwards she carefully kept the width of the room between us)—while, on the other hand, they never forget any little kindness, nor do they require to be reminded who are their friends.

"As another instance of their sagacity and retentive memory, some weeks previous to the show at Birmingham in 1876, where my bitch puppy Dora was entered, and only six months old, I was anxious to get a pair of her milk-teeth removed, and being very fast I did not like to venture on the operation myself, but took her to the shop of a dental friend, who removed them with very little trouble.

"I had forgotten all about the affair when I called at the same shop some twelve months afterwards. The little bitch was with me, but I missed her, and at last saw her skulking against a wall about forty yards away; and not being able to understand her movements, I called my friend, who immediately remarked, 'Why, it's the little dog I drew the teeth for, and she does not care for the operation.'

"They are excellent guards, and, being on such short legs, seem, from their nearness to the ground, to have a quicker sense of hearing, and I have frequently known them give the alarm some time before longer-legged dogs took any notice whatever of the sound.

"With dogs of their own variety they are generally very peaceable, and may easily be kept in bulk in kennels, but when they once quarrel they must be separated for ever as kennel companions, else one or other will be destroyed.

"With those of other breeds they are peculiar, never quarrelsome, and hardly ever are the first to begin a fight; but if attacked by a bigger dog they will not by any means hang back, and generally come off best, as they fight low, and work among their adversary's legs and throat; while a small dog, even if as big as themselves, they will often treat with supreme contempt.

"Festus was the foundation of my kennel of this breed, and is by Feldmann, out of an imported bitch of equal character. He was shown for two seasons only, is about seven years old, and scales 20 lbs. when in good condition; in colour a beautiful fallow-red. During this time he was the winner of forty-seven prizes and two cups, including two firsts and one cup at Birmingham, in 1875 and 1876."

Mr. Everett Millais, of Palace Gate, London, who has studied the breed most carefully, is entirely of Mr. Lovell's opinion on the question of head; and in answer to a question put to him by us with reference to his views on the subject, replies as follows:—

"What is a Dachshund?—A hound used on the Continent, more especially Germany, for the purpose of driving badgers and foxes from their underground lairs; also for the purpose of tracking and beating underwood above ground. Often and often am I asked whether I have seen so and so's hound, or if I will come and see one that another friend has imported. When I come home from the visit I think what money might have been saved if the purchaser had only gone to a Kennel Club show, paid his half-crown, and seen what constitutes a Dachshund.

"Of all people in this world John Bull abroad is the easiest to swindle. If he goes to Waterloo, bullets, &c., are imposed on him that never knew the battle-field. If to Germany, he is let in with some mongrel with crooked legs. Being an old breeder—and I may say a successful one, although I only showed one Dachshund in my life—I hope it will not be taken amiss if I say that 90 per cent. of the Dachshunds now seen in this city (of London) are no more the pure Dachshund they are represented to be than those mongrels in Paris that have the audacity to sign themselves Bull-terrier.

"There are certain breeders who, not having the courage to stick up for one legitimate type, excuse themselves by saying that there are two distinct types of Dachshunds—the Hound type and the Terrier type. This is a great and fatal mistake. That there are dogs, and alas, too many of them, with fine bone, Terrier sterns, Terrier heads, and light crooked legs, I will not deny; but, at the same time, I say that they are mongrels. They have got a root in this country, and it will always be my endeavour to eradicate it on every opportunity. The Dachshund proper is a hound, and a little beauty too. It is very easy to breed a Terrier from a hound, but it is impossible to breed a hound from a Terrier.

"The male Dachshund should weigh, when in proper condition, from 20 to 22 lbs.—certainly not more—and the female proportionately lighter. The head of the Dachshund should be conical, though not to such a marked degree as the Bloodhound. The ears are set on low, and hang like a hound's; they ought to reach some way over his nose. The Dachshund possesses a good flew, and a fair amount of jowl. His neck is extremely muscular, and should stand well out from the chest. The legs, which are one of the most important parts of a Dachshund, should come down from the chest, which is broad and massive, slope well towards one another till the ankle-joints nearly touch one another, the chest dropping down to the ankles. The fore-feet should, an inch from the chest, turn away from one another, and spread well out. On no account should the joints at the ankles have a forward bend, as it is unsightly, and shows a tendency to weakness.

"The stern is not carried over the back; this is a sure sign of the Terrier type. It is carried straight, with perhaps four inches elevation.

"A good hound should measure from 8½ to 10 inches in height, and from 36 to 38 inches in length. The skin should be loose all over the body, so that on grasping the hound you find you have a handful of skin. The hair should be hard, short, and glossy.

"Colour is an essential matter to the Dachshund. I myself care little whether it be red, black-and-tan, or chocolate-and-tan, but I will have a good colour. I do not care for white about the hound, for he is far better without it; but I would not disqualify him for having it were he otherwise good.

"In red dogs, and other than red, I much prefer red noses and eyes the colour of their coats, as I think it gives them a much more pleasing look.

"One sometimes sees a mottled species like a Collie with a wall eye. It looks very funny, but in my opinion it gets this from some other stock, not the hound."

Having thus given our readers the opinions of three leading English breeders upon the subject of Dachshunds, we will, before we attempt to sum up their ideas, give a list of points drawn up by some German breeders, which have been forwarded to us. This description was published at the time of the Hanover dog show, held in that city in 1879, and was much commented on when it first appeared. It is as follows:—

The principal qualities are—

1. *General appearance,* low and very long structure, overhanging and well-developed chest, legs very short, the fore-legs turned inwards at the knees, with the feet considerably bent out. The whole appearance is weasel-like; the tail is not much crooked, and is carried either straight or a little sloping. Hair close, short, and smooth; expression intelligent, attentive, and lively. Weight not over 10 kilos.

2. *Head* long and pointed towards the nose; forehead broad and flat; nose narrow; the lips hang over a little, and form a sort of fold in the corner of the mouth.

3. *Ears* of medium length, tolerably broad and round at the ends, placed high up and at the back of the head, so that the space between eye and ear appears considerably larger than with other hunting dogs; they are smooth and close, and droop with any shaking of the head.

4. *Eyes* not too large, round and clear, rather protruding, and very sharp in expression.

5. *Neck* long, flexible, broad, and strong.

6. *Back* very long, and broad in the hind parts.

7. *Breast* broad, ribs deep and very long, and back part of body higher than the front.

8. *Tail* of medium length, strong at the root, and gradually running to a short point, almost straight, occasionally with a small curve.

9. *Fore parts* much stronger than the hind, muscular shoulders, which are short; fore-quarter very short and strong, bending outwards, the knee inwards, and the feet again outwards.

10. *Hind legs*—knuckles strong and muscular; lower extremities very short, and quite in comparison with the front legs.

11. *Fore feet* much stronger than the hind feet, broad, and the toes well closed; the nails strong, uneven, and particularly of a black colour, with a strong sole to the feet. The hind feet are smaller and rounder, the toes and nails shorter and straighter.

12. *Hair* short, close, and glossy, smooth and elastic, very short and fine on the ears;

ROUGH-COATED DACHSHUNDS.

coarser and longer on the lower part of the tail. The hair on the lower part of the body is also coarser.

13. *Colour* black, with tan on the head, neck, breast, legs, and under the tail; besides dark-brown, golden-brown, and hare-grey, with darker stripes on the back; as also ash-grey and silver-grey, with darker patches (*Tigerdachs*). The darker colours are mostly mixed with tan and with the lighter colours; the nails ought to be black, and the eyes dark. White is only to be endured in the shape of a stripe on the chest straight down.

14. *Teeth.*—Upper and lower teeth meet exactly; they must be strong in every respect.

These dogs may be considered as *faulty* which have a *compressed or conical head*, if the nose is too short or too narrow, if the lips are too long, *long* faltering ears, thin neck and narrow chest, if the front legs are not regularly bent, or if the *crookedness of the legs is so strong as not to carry the weight* of the body. Further, the feet, if they are not regularly formed; if the hind legs are too long, and likewise the tail when too long and heavy and conspicuously crooked. With regard to colour, it is to be said that white as ground colour is also to be considered faulty, with the exception of what is mentioned before.

The task of attempting to decide where doctors have disagreed now falls upon our shoulders; for, as will have been seen above, the opinions we have quoted fail very much to coincide with one another. It has been our desire, however, in each and every instance, where we think a reasonable ground for difference of opinion exists, to give each side a full chance of publicity, and therefore we have devoted considerable space to the breed now under discussion. For our own part we are certainly in favour of the type supported by Messrs. Lovell and Millais, not out of any feelings of insular prejudice, but because we consider that type—the *hound* type—has been proved to be in existence for centuries. In the two earlier cuts of Dachshunds which accompany this article, and which are taken from *La Venerie*, by Jacques du Fouilloux, we notice most unmistakably that the dogs depicted are of the high conical skull which Mr. Lovell and Mr. Millais so stoutly maintain is the correct formation. Later on we come to a small cut from that *Icones Animalium* which has already been drawn upon to assist us in the present work. Here a very similar type of dog to those shown in *La Venerie* is produced, and the favourable impression towards the hound type is thereby much increased in our opinion. In estimating such matters, also, we cannot help thinking it advisable to turn one's thoughts in the direction of the uses to which a breed is put. In so doing, our views concerning the hound type have been greatly strengthened from the reflection that, as we have already said, tracking game is the Dachshund's forte, not baiting savage vermin in the latter's native earth. One remark, too, of Mr. Millais's has struck us very forcibly. "It is very easy to breed a Terrier from a hound, but it is impossible to breed a hound from a Terrier." Without going the entire length of Mr. Millais as to the impossibility of the latter achievement in breeding, we readily accept its difficulty, and recognise the force of the argument he makes use of.

We are not, however, wholly at one with Mr. Millais in his sweeping condemnation of the Terrier type. We prefer the hound type of Dachshund as being in our opinion the older and the more characteristic of the two; but in the face of what we have seen and heard, it is impossible to ignore the existence of the Terrier type, and the store set upon it in certain parts of its native country—Hanover to-wit. How this class of dog originated, except by crossing the hound type of Dachshund with a Terrier, we cannot tell; but as it now exists it is impossible to decline to recognise it as a variety, though perhaps an undesirable one, of the breed. A satisfactory illustration of this class of dog will be seen in the engraving, and our readers who are ignorant of the different types will thereby be able to form their own opinions on the beauty of the Terrier type of dog.

Another point on which Mr. Everett Millais and Mr. Enoch Hutton break a lance is that of the colour of the red Dachshund's nose. Here, as in Germany, considerable difference of opinion exists; but we personally feel no hesitation in offering our allegiance to the party which advocates red noses, as black noses in such cases look quite out of keeping with the colour.

There remains one description of Dachshund which has been quite overlooked by Messrs. Lovell, Millais, and Hutton, and which is rarely seen in this country, and that is the rough-coated variety, which will be found to be represented in the engraving on the preceding page. This breed, no doubt, is but a cross from the original variety, and is not valued in its native country by admirers of the breed.

DACHSHUND BREEDERS.

From what has been said and written concerning the breed from time to time by various authorities, it will be seen that it is not only on the subject of type that their admirers differ. Enthusiasts, as we have before remarked, give this breed of dog credit for an amount of gameness which we scarcely think it fully deserves. It is no doubt true that instances of exceptionally game Dachshunds have come beneath the observation of gentlemen who have studied the breed, as in the cases Mr. Enoch Hutton quotes; but we are inclined to imagine that these are exceptions rather than invariable rules. As house-dogs Dachshunds are without superiors, as their voices are deep enough to awaken the heaviest sleeper, and their sense of hearing is very acute.

In consequence of the fast-increasing number of these dogs which appear at the principal dog shows, efforts have been made to gain additional classes for them, as they are usually divided according to *colour* only. Classes for Dachshunds black-and-tan, and Dachshunds other than black-and-tan, have been up to the time of writing (1880) the order of the day, and no doubt during the earlier stages of this variety's existence as a show dog were amply sufficient. As, however, so many specimens of either type appear, certain exhibitors have been trying to gain classes for each variety of their favourite dog, with apparently some chance of ultimate success. The efforts of these breeders, however, are not regarded with favour by the supporters of the hound type of Dachshund, who maintain that the Terrier type is a mongrel unworthy of support, and therefore advocate the institution of heavy weight and light weight classes, instead of a division of the types. How things will work it is impossible to foretell; but an indisputable fact in connection with the Dachshund is its fast-increasing popularity amongst us, and its admirers appear to spare no trouble or expense in importing the best blood into the country.

Having now come to the end of our notes on the Dachshund, we can but once more repeat that our sympathies lie with the class of dog so ably depicted by the Rev. G. F. Lovell; but under any circumstances we would caution breeders against crossing the two types together, as certain ruin will be caused to each thereby. In breeding, we may remark that liver-coloured puppies frequently appear when reds are bred together. This colour, though disliked for show purposes, is often very valuable for crossing when increased depth of colour is required, and therefore a liver-coloured brood bitch or two is often seen in breeders' kennels. Whilst on this subject of colour we may remark that we cordially endorse the views already given on the subject of white. It is most undesirable that white blazes on the head or chest should ever be seen, and white feet we regard almost as a disqualification. In Germany we have seen many of the breed marked similarly to hounds, but cannot recall any to memory which were black-and-tans or fallow-reds marked with white. As regards the black ones, Mr. Mackenzie, of Perth, in 1879, imported a very handsome dog of this colour who rejoices in the name of Gravedigger. This dog was a good winner in his own country, and has done his master good service in the land of his adoption, and we do not know of a better-coated one, his skin being everything that could be desired.

Amongst the leading Dachshund breeders and exhibitors of the day the names of the Rev. G. F. Lovell, Mr. John Fisher, Mr. Everett Millais, Mr. W. Arkwright, and Mr. Enoch Hutton, are the most prominent, the first-named gentleman having been the owner of what is still considered to have been the best Dachshund ever seen in this country. We allude to Pixie, a wonderful little bitch, whose untimely death alone prevented her appearing in our coloured plate. Mr. John Fisher's Feldmann was truly, as Mr. Hutton says, the pioneer of his variety in this country, and Mr. Hutton's Festus, whose portrait is in our coloured plate, is recognised as a grand specimen of his type. Mr. Millais has not shown much, but has good dogs; and Mr. Arkwright's Xaverl was for a long time champion of his breed.

The dogs selected for illustration in the coloured plate are—

Major Cooper's (of Pitsford Hall, Northampton) Waldmann, an extremely good specimen of the black-and-tan variety, who is a winner at some of our best shows.

The Rev. G. F. Lovell's Schlupferle. A handsome fallow-red, whose measurements are as follows :—Length from tip of nose to stop, 3 inches; from stop to occiput, 4¾ inches; length of back from top of shoulders to setting on of stern, 16 inches; girth of thigh, 9 inches; girth of fore-arm, 5 inches; girth of pastern, 3½ inches; height at shoulders, 12 inches; height at elbows, 6½ inches; height at loins, 13½ inches; height at hock, 4½ inches; length of stern, 11 inches; weight, 23 lbs.; age, 4 years 10 months.

Mr. Enoch Hutton's Festus, already alluded to by his owner in the notes with which he obliged us as above.

The large full-page illustration of Dachshunds at work is the production of a celebrated foreign artist, who is especially happy in conveying the expression of animals to paper.

Following our usual custom, we shall now append a scale of points for judging the breed, which we cheerfully admit are founded upon the scale afforded us by Mr. Lovell in the preceding portion of this chapter :—

STANDARD OF POINTS FOR JUDGING DACHSHUNDS.

							Value.
Skull and muzzle	...	...	...	...	...	...	10
Ears and eyes ...	...	...	...	...	...	...	5
Shoulders and chest	...	...	...	...	...	...	5
Loins	...	...	...	...	...	...	5
Fore legs and feet	...	...	...	...	...	...	5
Hind legs and feet	...	...	...	...	...	...	5
Colour and coat...	...	...	...	...	...	...	5
General appearance, including skin		...	...	...	...		10
					Total ...	...	...	50

DACHSHUNDS.

CHAPTER XXIII

THE DACHSHUND

BEWICK says that the Kibble-hound of his day was a cross between the old English Hound and the Beagle, which would give a low hound, but not a swift one ; indeed, lowness and swiftness are incompatible. Whether the Dachshund is a Kibble-hound, or even what a Kibble-hound exactly was, is not very clear, for kennel terms vary greatly in meaning in course of time.

The word Dachshund means "badger dog," and not "hound," as that term is used by our hunting men. He has, however, notwithstanding his use as a Terrier, many of the properties of the hound, and varietally should be classed with them ; indeed, our own native Terriers are classed with the hounds by Caius, although many of our existing varieties are of very different type from hounds. The term "Kibble-hound" may have been applied to such as were short and crooked in the leg, as if broken, and, in that sense, the Dachshund, the Basset, and some of our Dandie Dinmont Terriers, may be called Kibble-hounds.

During the last few years Dachshunds have immensely increased in numbers. It is, however, doubtful whether as regards quality and character the dog has progressed with equal steps. In fact, the Dachshund is becoming more and more a fashionable pet than a workman—a quality with which the breed was associated when it was first introduced in this country.

The following was contributed to the First Edition of this work by "Vert," whose large experience of Dachshunds entitles his opinions on the breed to be considered authoritative :—

"So much has been said and written on this breed of dogs during the few years that they have had a place in the prize schedules of our shows, that in treating the subject we shall endeavour to unsay some of the nonsense that has from time to time been put forth by some of those journals whose pages are opened to the discussion of canine matters, in one of which a certain amusing correspondent, in a playful moment, tells his readers

15

that the ears of the Dachshund cannot be too long. Another says the body cannot be too long. Then we read that the legs cannot be too short or too crooked, with such impossible measurements as could only be found in the fertile brain of the writer. At shows we have had our special attention drawn to the veriest mongrels, and been held by the button by enthusiastic owners, and had glaring defects pointed out as characteristics of the pure breed; but, being unable to draw on our credulity to that extent, we have had to fall back on our stock of charity, and call to mind that even Solomon was young once in his lifetime. There is no breed of dogs that the English have been so tardy in taking to as the Dachshund, Satan and Feldmann being the only representatives of the breed on the Birmingham show-bench for several years; and certainly we had one judge who had the courage to grapple with this little hound when he did make an attempt to emerge from his obscurity, and we have seen the best Dachshund that has yet been exhibited passed over by a couple of 'all-round' judges of high standing at an important show, one of those Solons arguing that he was a Beagle Otter-hound, and the other that he was a Turnspit; neither of them being aware that the Turnspit was little different from a moderate crooked-legged Pug of the present time, and that it would be impossible to confine a long-backed twenty-pound dog in one of those small cages in which the little prisoner had to ply his calling. We have no wish to speculate on the early history of this breed, as, like other cases, it would be a mere leap in the dark from the same source as before alluded to. We have been seriously told that the breed came originally from France, and that once on a time, when the French army invaded Germany, and were capturing towns and provinces, the German nobles, by way of retaliation, invaded France and carried off all the Dachshunds; but as we do not find this theory supported by any authority that we have consulted, possibly the writer of the story may be entitled to the invention also.

The Dachshund is a short-coated, long-backed dog, on very short legs, of about 20lb. weight, and should not be less than 18lb., the bitches being 3lb. or 4lb. less than the dogs. They must be self-coloured, although a little white on the breast or toes should not be a disqualification, as these beauty spots will crop out now and then in any breed of dogs.

The colour most in fashion just now is the fallow red and black-and-tan, but we have very good specimens of various shades of red, more or less smutty, as well as the brown with tawny markings, some of which are very handsome. In black-and-tan we do not demand pencilled toes, as in the Terrier, although, if good in every other respect, we should consider it an acquisition; but we prefer such as nearest approach the standard of excellence, and care little for shades of colour, so that it be any of those above named. The head, when of the proper type, greatly resembles that of the Bloodhound. The ears also are long and pendulous, and in a 20lb. dog should measure from 4½in. to 5in. each, and from tip to tip over the cranium, when hanging down in their natural position, from 13in. to 14in. ; the length from the eye to the end of the nose should be over 3in., 3½in. being a good length for a dog of 20lb. weight ; girth of muzzle, from 8in. to 8½in., which should finish square, and not snipey or spigot-nosed, and the flews should be fairly developed ; the eyes should be very lustrous and mild in expression, varying in colour with that of the coat; the teeth should be very strong and perfectly sound, as a dog with a diseased mouth is of little use for work, is very objectionable as a companion, and is quite unfit for the stud in this or any other breed of dogs ; the neck should be rather long and very muscular. We have a brood bitch from one of the best kennels in Germany, in which the dewlap is very strongly pronounced; but this and the conical head are but rarely met with as yet. The chest should be broad, with the brisket point well up to the throat; the shoulders should be very loose, giving the chest an appearance of hanging between them ; they should be well covered with muscle, with plenty of loose skin about them. The fore legs are one of the great peculiarities of the breed ; these are very large in bone for the size of the dog, and very crooked, being turned out at the elbows and in at the knees ; the knees, however, should not 'knuckle,' or stand forward over the ankles, as we frequently see in very crooked-legged dogs, which renders them more clumsy and less powerful. The feet should be very large, and armed with strong claws, and should be well splayed outwards, to enable him to clear his way in the burrow. Terrier-like fore feet cannot be tolerated in the Dachshund, as great speed is not required, the great essentials being : a good nose for tracking ; a conformation of body that will admit of his entering the badger earth, and adapting himself to his situation ; and a lion heart and power to grapple with the quarry, in the earth or in the open—and these are no small requirements. We are frequently told So-and-so's Terrier has finished his badger in some very small number of minutes. But there are badgers and badgers—baby badgers ; and if we are to believe a tithe of what we hear on this head, the supposition is forced upon us that a great many badgers die in their infancy.

We do know that the premier Dachshund of the present day has drawn a wild fox from his fastness, and finished him, unaided, in about four minutes ; but an unsnubbed, fully matured badger of five or six summers is an awkward customer, and with him the result might have been quite different.

What are called Dachshunds may be picked up in most

German towns; but those are often of an inferior sort, or half-breds, the genuine blue blood being almost entirely in the hands of the nobles. Familiar to us in the north were those of the late King of Hanover; those of Baron Nathasius and Baron Von Cram in the south. The Grand Duke of Baden's kennel, at Eberstein Schloss, is unrivalled. Prince Couza, Baroness Ingelheim, and Baron Haber also possessed some of the best and purest strains.

In England Her Majesty the Queen and H.S.H. Prince Edward of Saxe-Weimar for many years possessed the choicest specimens of the best strains in Germany; and we have been favoured with stud dogs and brood from some of the above-named kennels, which required something more than gold to possess them. A habit has sprung up of late—and a very bad one it is— of entering rough-coated little dogs as Dachshunds at some of our best shows, and some of them have received honours which they are in no way entitled to. This is misleading, as they are not Dachshunds, but 'Bassets'—very nice little fellows, but with no more right to be exhibited as Dachshunds than a Setter or a Spaniel would have in a Pointer class. They may be half-breds— as Dachshund-Basset or Dachshund-Spaniel. We have also met with others, hound-marked and smooth-coated, which looked like Dachshund-Beagles; these are all Bassets, a term applied by the French to all low, short-legged dogs. The best we have met with were a leash owned by a French marquis; these had grand heads of the Otter-hound type, with rough coats, very long bodies, and short, crooked legs, and were called 'Rostaing Bassets,' and were excellent workers in thick coverts; but they rarely possess either the courage or the scenting powers of the Dachshund."

Having quoted the opinions of a well-known authority in the early show days of the variety, we now give the opinions of a present-day enthusiast in the breed, Mr. Harry Jones, and one whose opinions, alike as breeder, exhibitor, and judge, are entitled to respect :—

" I do not propose in any way to deal with the ancient history of the Dachshund, but simply to write about Dachshunds as we have known them in England since they have been exhibited at our dog shows. Strange as it may appear, a separate class for this breed was given at the Crystal Palace Show in 1873, five years before the earliest record of a separate class being given for Dachshunds at a dog show in their native country—viz. at Berlin in 1878 (see Vol. I. of the 'Teckel-Stammbuch,' published by the 'Teckel-Klub' in 1891).

During the seventies the numbers of Dachshunds seen at our best shows rapidly increased, and Mr. W. Schuller, of Poland Street,

imported a considerable number of the winners of the day ; but the
two Dachshunds, imported about this time, to whom most of the
modern Dachshunds can be traced back were Waldine (6,355)
and Xaverl (6,337), the former being the dam of Chenda (6,339),
Hans (8,380), Zanah (8,404), etc., and the latter the sire of Hans
(8,380), Zigzag (8,393), etc. etc. The latter's son Ozone (10,502) sired
the two brothers Maximus (12,767) and Superbus (12,776), probably
the most successful show and stud dogs of the breed in this country,
but they owed a great deal of their success to their dam Thusnelda
(10,528), imported by Mr. W. Schuller. She was first exhibited by
Mr. Mudie at the Kennel Club Show of 1880. She was smaller than
most of the Dachshunds then being shown, and was stated to have
won several first prizes at Continental shows. She proved to be
the most valuable importation of all the Dachshunds that passed
through the hands of Mr. Schuller. Although she left no progeny
in Mr. Mudie's kennel, she bred most successfully to both Ozone
and Wag when in Mr. Arkwright's kennel.

There is no doubt that nearly all our Dachshunds that were too
large and houndy in type obtained this from the strain of Waldine
(6,355), but this strain when crossed with Thusnelda soon produced
the right size and the type required.

In January, 1881, the Dachshund Club was formed, and before
the end of the year a description of the Dachshund with a scale of
points was published. It has often been stated that the Dachshund
Club when it published the description of the variety did so in
direct opposition to the acknowledged German type ; but the writers
who make these statements surely overlook the fact that this
standard was compiled in England and published ten years before
any standard or scale of points were published by any acknowledged
German authority—viz. the Teckel-Klub in 1891.

The standard described the Dachshund as he was then known
in this country by the imported dogs that were being exhibited,
and that were stated to have won prizes before being imported, and
to have been bred in the very best German kennels ; but there is no
doubt whatever that these imported dogs were more houndy in type
than the Dachshund described in the scale of points published by
the Teckel-Klub ten years later.

Although the points of the breed as published by the two clubs
had important differences, there was not so much difference in the
type of the dogs themselves.

In 1882 Dachshunds that were prize winners at our shows, and
bred from the most successful winners of the day, competed successfully at Hanover under a German judge.

In 1885 and 1886 I exhibited Wagtail (16,633)—a daughter
of Thusnelda, and the dam of Jackdaw (20,689), the most successful English-bred Dachshund ever exhibited—at the shows of the

St. Hubert Society, under a German judge, and each year she not only won the first prize in her class, but was awarded the *prix d'honneur* for the best Dachshund of all classes. She was a small-sized black-and-tan.

In 1891 I exhibited Pterodactyl (24,854) at Spa under a German judge, who awarded him first prize in his class, but he was not permitted to compete for the *prix d'honneur ;* and Pterodactyl was one of the most successful prize winners in England.

That Dachshunds of very different types do win prizes under our different judges is only what occurs in nearly every breed of dog ; but since the Teckel-Klub published its scale of points there has been a decided effort on the part of English breeders to breed more on the lines of the best of the German dogs, and with this object several of the winning dogs at the trials and shows have been imported during the last few years.

I think the greatest harm that is now being done to the breed in England is to change the nature of the dog, from being a hardy, keen, sporting little dog, quite able to hold his own with any dog of his size at field sports, into the ladies' pet dog we now find him. Instead of being a merry, bold, active dog in the ring, we find half of them are so shy that they cannot be induced to walk, and some will not even stand up.

That the Dachshund in his native country is a game sporting little dog will be admitted by all who have seen the trials under ground at foxes and badgers at Continental shows. Nearly all the prize winners were good workers, and some were excellent under ground.

I think it is a far more serious matter to change this sporting little companion from a hardy, courageous dog into a pet dog, nervous, delicate, and shy, than to have a difference in the scale of points."

No less interesting and practical are the opinions expressed by another well-known breeder of the variety, Mr. J. F. Sayer. That gentleman, in his review of the breed in the *Kennel Gazette* of January, 1903, states that :—

" What we want now is a few good German-bred dogs for mating with our houndy bitches to produce better stamina and courage, better legs and feet, tails, skin, and colour. The body and chest we have fairly right, and even the head, as to skull, etc., but stronger jaws are required. I have been much impressed when judging by the comparatively few Dachshunds that are really sound on their legs and able to stand evenly on their feet. Many can stand without knuckling over ; but soundness demands something more exacting than this—namely, strong (sound) feet, not too long, outspreading, and not twisted. The twisted foot is oftenest observed, and no dog with such a fault can be considered absolutely sound. Then, again, another striking fault, though not, I believe, so damning as unsoundness, is the loose shoulder—out-at-elbow— a sign of weakness in a most vital part of a Dachshund. How rarely one sees a good level back, with proper loin development ! A great number of present-day winners dip behind the shoulders, and perhaps more are higher on quarters than at shoulder.

Muscle is absolutely at a discount, and its place is taken by beefiness. I wonder how many of our show dogs get more than

FIG. 55.—MISS A. M. PIGOTT'S DACHSHUND CHAMPION PRIME MINISTER.

the minimum allowance of exercise, to say nothing of work. . . . Sterns must not be neglected—curly tails, sausage tails, crooked tails, etc., are all only too apparent ; but the correct tail—not too long, strong at base, tapering gradually to the top, and moderately feathered underneath—how few do we see ! Skin of the right texture we neglect, or perhaps I should say we are losing it, in spite of ourselves, by inbreeding. The Dachshund should have plenty of thick skin, but it should be thick and covered with hair that, on being stroked the wrong way is resisting to the touch, instead of soft and yielding. Colour is rapidly fading. Red dogs are nowadays chiefly yellow, shading to whitish fawn. The beautiful cherry-red is rarely seen, and the black-and-tan is almost conspicuous on the benches on account of its unusual colour! Even the black-and-tan is losing its rich tan markings, and a lot of half-and-half colours are cropping up. Colour is certainly a minor point; but it helps to illustrate my contention that an outcross is desirable. We have long ago exploded the theory of classifying Dachshunds by colour, but there is much to be said for the care with which the Germans have preserved the colour pure. I think that we might with advantage take a leaf out of their book by classifying our dogs by weight, for the variation in size and weight of our leading winners is most extraordinary, and must be very bewildering to beginners, and even to older hands. . . . The right size and weight for a Dachshund is about 18lb. for bitches, and a couple of pounds heavier for dogs."

The practical breeder will do well to carefully digest what Mr. Sayer has written with regard to the Dachshund, for they are words of wisdom, though uttered none too soon.

Though the Dachshund (Fig. 55) in this country is not called upon, as a rule, to "work," yet occasionally we find an owner who takes a wholesome pride in those qualities that so endear the breed to its Continental admirers. We have more than once seen the working qualities of the variety put to practical test. To the fact that as a mere ornament it is of greater monetary value than as a utility animal must be ascribed the apathy exhibited by owners with regard to its working qualities; for to develop the latter to the full would be to put the dog out of court for show-bench honours. The Dachshund, taken generally, makes an ideal companion and house-guard; while it is one of the easiest of dogs to keep in first-class condition.

The matter we have quoted from Mr. J. F. Sayer's very practical contribution to the periodical above referred to sufficiently indicates the lines that the novice should go upon when selecting a dog, especially when taken in conjunction with the description of the breed furnished by the Dachshund Club and given below and the illustration that accompanies this chapter. "Vert," in his contribution at the beginning of this chaper, disapproves of the Rough-haired Dachshund; and the only addition that calls for mention in connection with the Club's description is the fact that dappled specimens are occasionally found and special classes provided for them at the larger shows.

The Dachshund standard, as settled by the Dachshund Club, November, 1881, is as follows :—

Head and Skull.—Long, level, and narrow; peak well developed; no stop; eyes intelligent and somewhat small; follow body in colour.

Ears.—Long, broad, and soft ; set on low, and well back ; carried close to the head.

Jaw.—Strong, level, and square to the muzzle ; canines recurvent.

Chest.—Deep and narrow ; breast-bone prominent.

Legs and Feet.—Fore legs very short, and strong in bone, well crooked, not standing over ; elbows well clothed with muscle, neither in nor out ; feet large, round, and strong, with thick pads and strong nails. Hind legs smaller in bone and higher, hind feet smaller. The dog must stand true—*i.e.* equally on all parts of the foot.

Skin and Coat.—Skin thick, loose, supple, and in great quantity ; coat dense, short, and strong.

Loin.—Well arched, long, and muscular.

Stern.—Long and strong, flat at root, tapering to the tip ; hair on under side coarse ; carried low, except when excited. Quarters very muscular.

Body.—Length from back of head to root of stern two and a half times the height at shoulder. Fore ribs well sprung, back ribs very short.

Colour.—Any colour ; nose to follow body colour ; much white objectionable.

Symmetry and Quality.—The Dachshund should be long, low, and graceful, not cloddy.

Weight.—Dogs, about 21lb. ; bitches, about 18lb.

SCALE OF POINTS

Head and Skull	...	...	...	...	...	12
Ears ...	...	...	...	...	...	6½
Jaw ...	...	...	...	...	...	5
Chest	...	...	...	...	...	7
Legs and Feet ...	...	...	...	...	...	20
Skin and Coat ...	...	...	...	...	...	13
Loin ...	...	...	...	...	...	8
Stern ...	...	...	...	...	...	5
Body ...	...	...	...	...	...	8½
Colour	...	...	...	...	...	4
Symmetry and Quality ...	...	...	...	...	...	11
		Total	...	...	...	100

The Dachshund Club states. that it does not advocate point judging, the figures given being only used to show the comparative value of the features.

The Dachshund is one of the few varieties that can boast a Stud Book of its own. "Dachshund Pedigrees" are monumental volumes, and bear eloquent testimony to the painstaking care and research bestowed upon them by their compilers, Mr. E. S. Woodiwiss and Mr. E. Watlock Allen. They contain a list of all registered Dachshunds up to date, giving their reputed sires and dams, dates of birth, colour, breeders, owners, etc. Apart, too, from the pedigrees, there are a number of admirable reproductions in black and white of "pillars of the Stud Book," English and German dogs alike. Such a feature will be a valuable one to the breeder in the future, who will not only be able to refer to the family tree, but also to see some splendid representations of animals forming its chief branches.

In the volumes referred to, which should be in the possession of every one interested in the Dachshund, occur of course the names of those fanciers who have done most to place the variety upon the pinnacle of fame it now enjoys. Already some of these have been mentioned, but there are some few others who, having espoused the cause of the variety on its introduction, have retained at least their affection for it up to the present day—Mr. A. O. Mudie, Mr. A. W. Byron, Mr. Montague Wootten, Mr. E. S. Woodiwiss, Miss Pigott, Mr. W. Arkwright, Captain and Mrs. Barry, and a few others; while the lady who at the outset was largely responsible for the dog's introduction here was Mrs. Merrick-Hoare.

To those accustomed to regard the soft-eyed, smooth-coated Dachshund as but a pampered pet-dog, incapable of little beyond the bestowal of its affection upon its owner and it may be the guarding of the house, the instructive contribution from Mr. William Carnegie ("Moorman") on the dog's working capabilities will come as a revelation. It is also to be hoped that those who have the true welfare of the breed at heart—and their name is legion—will see fit to pay attention to those workmanlike qualities that first endeared the breed to English hearts, instead of contriving to breed solely for those more ornamental ones that fickle Fashion has for the nonce ruled shall obtain :—

" The popularity of the Dachshund in this country dates now for many years back, but the curious little dogs have never achieved that position for either Terrier or Hound work that they hold in Germany, Austro-Hungary, and other parts of the Continent. They quickly secured the approval of the ' Fancy ' upon introduction to English kennels and the benches of our dog shows ; but to a very large, in fact, preponderating, extent their merits in field and covert, when properly trained and worked, have been either overlooked or ignored. True, there have been, and are, many owners of Dachshunds who have sought to prove their worth otherwise than as merely fancy dogs ; but whatever measure of success has crowned their efforts in this direction, the generality of those interested in the breed have not sought to follow up or extend these favourable results.

No doubt the name Dachshund, with the German translation of ' badger-dog,' has handicapped the breed for work in this country, because people naturally point to the scarcity of badgers in most parts of the British Isles, and, further, to the apparent unsuitability of the undoubtedly peculiarly built dogs for drawing badgers, their inability to tackle them, and the pronounced fact that we have numberless dogs of various Terrier breeds more suitable to work of this kind than the Dachshund itself.

It is greatly to be regretted that the breed has been so closely and so solely associated with the badger by those who patronise and stand fast by the breed. This is not the case in the Continental countries, where it chiefly predominates, and where its name has become more familiar in the semi-diminutive, semi-nicknames of Daxel or Teckel. Had the dog come to us under any other name than Dachshund, and its inevitable translation of ' badger-dog,' there would seem to be every reason to believe it would have taken better place as a worker than it has done so far.

To properly appreciate the position that the Dachshund holds in the countries that chiefly esteem it, it is necessary for the un-acquainted British amateur to compare it with the position held by some of our Terrier breeds. It is unnecessary to particularise ; but for the present purpose any popular breed of working Terrier may be taken as representative. In these islands we should have a standard of excellence which would govern the positions of the best-bred dogs at shows and elsewhere, a general type of well-bred members of the breed, and the usual mongrel riff-raff; we should have dogs bred and kept mainly for showing, others for pets or companions, and others bred and maintained solely for work in the special direction and under the special conditions demanded by various circumstances. Such is precisely the position of the Dachshund in the Continental countries named ; but it holds an additional one, possessed by no other single breed in the British Isles—it is essentially the companion of the sportsman, the woods-man, and the gamekeeper. Whatever the resources of the kennels of the one or the other, one or more Dachshunds seem to be a *sine quâ non*, and in the vast majority of cases the Daxel or Teckel will be a useful, well-trained dog, well up to any of the chance work such as a gamekeeper or a sportsman would come across in going his rounds, or in an ordinary stroll over the preserve with dog and gun.

This class of Dachshund serves as a sort of general utility dog. If a hare or a rabbit be wounded by a shot, the dog will find or retrieve it ; a varmint be found in a trap, it will kill it ; if there be fur or feather to be found and driven from covert, the dog is trained and is quite equal to the task.

These are all services such as one can command from one or other of our own breeds of dogs employed for sport ; but then a single properly trained Dachshund will perform them all, whilst the little hounds may also be trained to work more associated with their name, and which I shall describe in detail later on.

It has been made clear so far that the Dachshund is capable of work in wood, covert, or field, of no mean order, and it is now necessary to see how these faculties for work can be developed. To this end we must take some stock of the breed as we now possess it. Those who are responsible for the type of Dachshund have frequently disputed between what may be termed Hound and Terrier type, and in this respect we find one of the causes of the fallacy which the name Dachshund begets influencing judgment in the wrong direction. The Dachshund never was a Terrier in the sense that we understand it of a dog for going to ground. True, well-trained ones—trained, that is, for this particular work—will go to ground and tackle fox or badger in its earth ; but the Dachshund, as a working dog, is and must be regarded in the light of a diminutive hound, working slowly, but steadily, by scent mostly, and driving game or vermin to the gun.

There are few dogs more sure or persistent upon a cold trail or scent ; they will follow and find wounded fur and feather where smarter breeds, such as a Spaniel or a Terrier, will over-run the quarry and remain at fault ; they will also, when worked in company, follow, worry, and bring to gun or to bay far superior quarry to dogs of their own weight and size of Terrier breed.

It will therefore be seen that to promote and thoroughly bring out the working capabilities of the Dachshund, it is, to say the least, unwise to attempt to enter them upon the same lines as one would commence the education of young Terriers. It is precisely for this reason that so many failures to make good working Dachshunds have resulted.

For a portion of its work a Dachshund requires to be entered upon the same lines as the small Beagles—Beagles, that is, of about 14in., not the oversized ones, neither Beagle, Harrier, nor Hound, of 17in. to even 19in., whose size and speed are too great for one style of work and insufficient for the other. Coupled with this form of work, the Dachshund requires entering also to that portion of a sporting Terrier's work that embraces the search by scent for fur or vermin, the driving of them to gun, net, or earth, but not the actual going to earth. When Dachshunds are required to go to earth after fox or badger, whether to tackle the quarry and hold it at bay till it is dug out, or to drive it from its burrow, a specific form of training is required—upon the same lines as the low-legged Scottish Terriers are entered for work amongst the cairns and rocky grounds of our northern province where foxes are shot and caught, but not hunted with hounds.

Slow seek, sure find, is the maxim that must guide the hand that seeks to train Dachshunds to the work of which they are capable and at which they are adepts. They cannot at their best replace any of our Terrier breeds at the work at which they in their turn are *facile princeps*, but they can be brought to such a state of serviceable training in the directions which have been mentioned as will freely prove their utility and value as an addition to our list of sporting dogs. The great point is that they must receive a special course of training suited to their peculiarities of form and nature and with a due appreciation of their possible powers. Of course, the general scheme of game-preservation and woodcraft in these islands is not the same as in the far larger and wilder lands of the countries where the Dachshund is chiefly valued and used, whilst at the same time the quarry upon which they can be worked is of far more limited character and variety. At the same time, the opportunities for employing them when properly trained are many and varied, as will be seen from the experiences of their working gained in those Continental districts where they are chiefly valued, and which will be described.

To properly appreciate what well-trained Dachshunds are capable of, it is necessary to have witnessed them at work, and shared in the sport in which their services are brought to bear. Given a concise insight into the manner in which they are employed abroad—admittedly under somewhat different circumstances from those obtaining at home—the outcome of the training to which they are submitted will serve as a guide to the possibilities of their use in our own lands.

For the most part the majority of the forests and woodlands of Germany harbour many more hares than do any of our British woods and coverts ; and in districts where the Dachshund is a plentiful feature of the kennels, it is freely employed for the purpose of beating out the hares for the individual gunner, or for general beats, where several sportsmen are concerned. These woodland hares do not strike straight away when started from their forms, but display very much the same tactics as rabbits, dodging here and there amongst the undergrowth where such exists, and confining their course to lesser and more circling limits where the woods are clear and the view of the quarry is more extended.

Under these conditions the work of the Dachshund upon hares resembles very much that of a steady, slow Spaniel—less bustling and headstrong, and running more by scent than sight when once the quarry is sighted. Along drives and paths Dachshunds learn to.work the ground on either side, never going deep into cover, but driving the hares to the open ground, where opportunity for shooting is greater. Many Dachshunds trained to this work will follow and retrieve a wounded hare—wounded heavily, that is, for it stands to reason that a Dachshund's pace would not be equal to running down one only slightly touched—within reasonable limits of time. Still, for all that, these dogs, when keen and thoroughly trained, are quite capable of such work, and many instances of their powers in this direction have come under my personal notice.

From the humane point of view this is a distinct merit, for the Dachshund is powerfully mawed, and makes no great fuss of cleanly killing a wounded hare and bringing it to bag. Of course we could find very little occasion for employing this breed for similar purposes in this country ; but in connection with that form of sport known as hedge-popping, Dachshunds would serve wonderfully well if properly trained to the work, and would probably furnish better sport than many of the Terriers and Spaniels usually brought into this style of work, frequently to their detriment for that of a more legitimate description.

Naturally chief interest in the Dachshund and its work must centre upon what dogs of the breed can do in connection with the badger. To rightly appreciate the working of any dog on badgers, it must be borne in mind that it must be specially entered for tackling or driving out these vermin. None of our British breeds is in itself specially constituted for this work ; but individual members, possessing the natural ability and disposition, figure prominently for the purpose. In just the same way, many Dachshunds are specially entered and worked upon badgers. These animals are very plentiful in many districts of Germany, but are wonderfully so upon some of the Hungarian slopes of the Carpathian Mountains. Properly trained Dachshunds are employed to hunt them to their lairs, as well as to go to earth, and either hold them in their burrows or drive them from them, when they are taken alive or shot, as the case may be.

Without going into details of the badger's merits or failings as an object of sport, or enlarging upon the details of the subject, it must, however, be pointed out that the habits of the brock are mainly nocturnal ; consequently the services of Dachshunds in this respect must be attuned to the nature of the work required. The badger, seemingly a clumsy animal, can, however, go at a comparatively speaking great rate ; it follows, therefore, that any dog capable of dealing with it in the open must not only possess a certain turn of speed, but be able to cope with the varmint if it comes up with it, or if the latter should turn upon its pursuer. These conditions the Dachshund is freely capable of fulfilling, and to far better advantage than the more speedy Terriers, whilst being at the same time better provided for tackling them, if it come to such necessity.

In those particular parts of the Carpathians to which reference has been made, the lower fringe of forest-land abuts right on to the higher slopes of cultivated land, where maize is largely grown. The badgers, which are remarkably numerous in these woods, are also bad enemies of the growing maize-crop, and will commit very serious depredations amongst it just before the time of harvest. The badgers will find their way down from their haunts at dusk, and, getting amongst the maize, pursue quite a devastating course. The expanses of growing corn are at times very considerable, and to deal successfully with the vermin—for such they are—many Dachshunds are employed. The routine is to put the dogs in upon them, and the men with the guns—proprietors, foresters, or watchers, as the case may be—take up positions between the growing crops and the wood-land; and as the dogs drive the badgers out, and the latter seek to reach their proper haunts, some are shot, and some are collared and killed by the Dachshunds.

It is found that no variety of dog is nearly so successful in this work as the Dachshund. His manner of working upon the badgers —chiefly by scent and sound—amongst the strong stalks of the maize is exactly that which seems most effective in getting them out and bringing them into the open ground, where they can be satisfactorily dealt with. There is a considerable element of sport and excitement about the whole business; and although it is not unusual for an occasional dog to get severely mauled, still, as a general rule the dogs have the best of it, and the procedure indicated is found to be the most effective to employ in dealing with the circumstances described. It is obvious that the counterpart of this form of work for the Dachshund exists to only very small extent in Great Britain; but there are certain districts where badgers are still fairly plentiful, and where a certain recognised form of sport is obtained in hunting them upon similar lines at night-time. As a rule, however, the badgers are either taken alive, or simply hunted back to their earths.

I believe I am correct in stating that a few years back a small pack of Dachshunds were successfully worked in connection with badger-hunting of this description; and it is perfectly certain that some of the small hounds, properly entered and trained to this work, would show more extended and better sport than would Terriers employed for the same purpose. At the same time, if required to go to ground, the Dachshund is far superior for the work to Terriers of either large or small breed: the former are too heavy and upstanding for work on badgers below ground, and the smaller ones, be the individual members never so plucky or hard, not by nature suited for dealing with such a foe. The badger is in many ways a naturally inoffensive creature, and from the humane standpoint, if it be necessary to draw or kill it, it is surely preferable to adopt the speediest and least cruel manner of so doing.

Those who know the Dachshund best would never seek to place its work upon rabbits in front of that of either Terriers or Spaniels, except as a mere set-off against or as a comparison with the work of these breeds. It is true enough that under certain conditions the Dachshund would prove superior; but these conditions are exceptional, and the colour of the breed is against it when working upon fur in close cover.

As furnishing an insight to the extreme possibilities of these little dogs, it may be mentioned that a well-known sportsman of my acquaintance, very keen on deer and ibex shooting in high grounds, has a couple of Dachshunds that he employs upon his stalks for tracking wounded quarry. He has found them to work with the greatest sureness upon comparatively cold scent, and save him many a head which otherwise might never have been brought to bag.

In conclusion, it may be remarked that the proper entering and training of Dachshunds to any of the work of which they are capable is a quite easy proceeding. They are extremely intelligent, and probably the least nervous, as a breed, of any dogs employed for similar purposes. The main point is to observe that they are not Terriers ; that the course of entering them to any quarry must be upon nearly the same lines as are adapted to the entering of Beagles or other small hounds ; that it is only sure and steady, but not necessarily slow, work of which they are capable. With these reservations, there is no reason why great numbers of the Dachshunds now existing in this country should not become as useful members of our kennels as are their congeners in Continental countries.

"IT is surprising how soon a want of care, or care wrongly directed, leads to the degeneracy of a domestic race." Thus speaks Mr. Darwin in his "Descent of Man," and no practical breeder of any sort of stock can be found to disagree with him. No care and attention on the part of the owner and his servants can turn a badly-bred, ill-formed animal into a good one; and though it is impossible to bestow too much consideration on the treatment of the stock, all exertions on behalf of animals badly bred will be, as a rule, thrown away when they come before the judge. Years of anxiety go for nothing, if due attention is not paid not only to the health and strength, but also to the proper selection of the breeding stock. As in the articles on the various breeds full prominence has been given to the special points which must be studied in each individual variety, it is unnecessary here for us to go beyond a general outline of the management of what may be called the breeding materials.

It is wonderful to reflect upon the success which seems to attend the efforts of some of the most loosely-conducted establishments, and to see winner after winner turned out from a kennel where no rules of breeding are for a moment studied, and where the management is often left by the owner in the hands of a kennel-man whose knowledge of the breed is absolutely *nil*. Such success in the few instances in which it occurs is eventually unfortunate in its results, both to the breeders of the dogs themselves and also to many of the outside world, who, either to save themselves trouble, or through ignorance of the simplest principles of breeding, ignorantly rush for the services of the nearest prize-winner, utterly regardless as to whether he is likely to "nick" with the bitch they propose uniting with him, in shape, size, or pedigree. The result may be a temporary success, but is certain ultimate destruction of all type. Breeding *can* be regulated by rules and judicious selection, else how do we see so many breeds of dogs now in existence (which we can prove to have originated from a cross of two older varieties) keep on throwing puppies which consistently resemble their parents in every property, and whose difference from them only consists in minor insignificant and immaterial features? By rigidly adhering to an ideal type, and resisting all temptations to go from it, a breeder is certain in time to find himself in possession of the sort of dog he has, rightly or wrongly, determined on possessing; and then he is in a position to discover, from the success of his dogs, whether his exertions are to be repaid or not.

We must commence, then, by impressing upon all beginners, and many older hands, the desirability of adhering to *one type* if they want to make a name for themselves as amateur breeders. Of course, in the case of those who breed solely for the market it is right that they should produce good specimens of every recognised standard, so as to please buyers, whatever their own opinions may be; but as these remarks are not intended to be addressed to dealers, who are perfectly competent to manage their own business, but to amateurs, it is sufficient to point out the importance of adhering to one type. By breeding to one standard, we necessarily imply that no one should be induced to set up as a producer of canine stock until he has clearly made up his mind what sort of animal he wishes for. In the case of a beginner, there is generally an acquaintance at hand who possesses more or less experience in such matters, and who, if he be a real lover of the dog, will be glad to place his services at his young friend's disposal. The opinions of such an individual may not all be correct; but if he be fairly competent, and honest, he can always be useful to the beginner. It is a great assistance, too, in arriving at a correct opinion, if the uses for which the various breeds have been brought into existence are brought under consideration. It is no good breeding a dog, though he be ever so handsome-looking, if he is palpably unfit for the work he is supposed to perform if called upon ; and, under a judge who knows his work, a flashy-looking dog often has to lower his colours to his more sober and workman-like neighbour, whose undoubted good properties have escaped the attention of the uninitiated.

Having decided upon the type which he himself desires to produce, a beginner should make it his next business to ascertain if his ideas in any way resemble the orthodox standard ; if so, his labours are considerably diminished, as his object in breeding will be to obtain the services of such stud dogs as he particularly admires, and in whose pedigree he has satisfied himself there is no bar sinister. It is an indisputable fact that a well-bred dog is far more likely to beget stock resembling himself than a good-looking mongrel is. Again, in the case of the former, even if he fails to impress his own likeness on his progeny, there is a possibility, if not a fair amount of certainty, that the puppies will throw back to a well-bred ancestor of more or less elegant proportions ; whilst with a dog whose pedigree is enveloped in mystery or something worse, there is a chance of the young ones displaying every conceivable type and temper.

The subject of in-breeding is one which has exercised the minds of breeders for many a day, and affords matter for a controversy which seems far from being brought to a termination. There can be no sort of doubt that, if carried to too great a length, in-breeding stunts the growth and weakens the intelligence and constitution of all dogs. This opinion is, we believe, unanimously received by all breeders of canine stock ; though, in the case of game-cocks more than one authority has it that incestuously-bred birds are stouter, gamer, and more active than those whose parents are unrelated to each other. Observation has proved that the union of father with daughter and mother with son is far preferable, where dogs are concerned, to an alliance between brother and sister. Once in and twice out is, we believe, an excellent system if the crosses are judiciously selected, and the reasons for this appear to be as follows :— A breeder has a dog belonging to a strain which usually produces good-headed ones, but apt to be leggy and perhaps deficient in coat. He naturally wishes to remedy these defects, and in many instances selects as a mate a dog indifferent in head, but good in bone and in jacket ; the result being most probably one fair puppy and several very indifferent ones which inherit the faults of both their sire and dam. On the other hand, however, had he exercised a little patience, and mated his dog with one of the same strain, thereby strengthening the probability of the puppies being in their turn likely to beget good-headed offspring when allied with another strain of blood, he would, in the course of a few years, have most probably got exactly the sort of dog he desired to obtain. We are perfectly aware that this argument may be said to cut both ways, and that those taking a contrary view of the case to our own may exclaim that the faults are just as likely to be perpetuated as the good properties; but we would observe that perpetual wandering from one blood to another *must* eventually produce specimens of uncertain type, whose services at the stud are perfectly useless from the fact that there is no fixed character in their breeding, and who are liable to throw puppies of every conceivable shape and make in the same litter. In short, in-breeding is, when judiciously carried out, absolutely essential to a breeder's success as a breeder, if such is to be maintained.

Finally, before closing our remarks upon the general subject of breeding, we wish to warn beginners that they are undertaking a tedious and very disappointing pursuit when they set up to be breeders of exhibition dogs. The best of calculations are often upset by accident or fate, and many a promising puppy falls a victim to the ills that puppyhood is peculiarly heir to. To have bred a first-rate dog of any breed is indeed a thing to be proud of, when it is considered how many scores of persons are expending time and money and judgment upon this very object. How few champions there are in the world is a statement which can be read in two ways—either there are so few that it should be an easy matter to add to their number ; or it may be construed as implying that a vast amount of labour is wasted in trying to produce what is in reality a matter of chance. To us there appears to be both truth and untruth in each opinion ; but the fact remains that champions have arisen, and will arise again, and are far more likely to be brought into existence when due attention is paid to the mates a breeder selects for his dogs.

Careful people invariably keep regular stud books referring to their breeding operations ; in these the date of birth (and if necessary of the purchase), colour, sex, weight, breeder, and performances of their stock, are registered. The visits of their own bitches, and of others to their stud dogs, are also entered ; as are the dates of sales, and the names and addresses of the purchasers. By this means ready and accurate information can be obtained concerning the history of any animal which may at one time or other pass through their hands.

THE STUD DOG.

A great deal of a breeder's success depends upon the state of health in which the stud dog is when he begets offspring ; for a delicate or unhealthy dog is more than likely to transmit his defects to his puppies, who are in consequence more difficult to rear, and of less value when they attain maturity. Considerable attention should therefore be paid to the comfort of a dog who is in the habit of receiving a large number of stud visits. He should, if possible, be well exercised morning and evening, either by a country walk, or a run round his owner's yard ; and his diet must be wholesome and liberal. A plunge in cold water materially assists in keeping a dog in vigorous condition, and in warm weather may be taken daily. It should be borne in mind, too, that it is always well to have your stud dogs look clean and tidy, both when out of doors and when in the kennels. Much depends upon the first impressions formed by the owner of a bitch who contemplates breeding from him, and many a dog is passed over whose services, had he been in better fettle, might have been resorted to. Care should be taken not to overtax the energies of a young sire by allowing him to receive too many stud visits ; the result of excesses in this way being both sickly offspring and his own ultimate failure at the stud. Fifteen or twenty bitches a year are quite enough for a dog not in his prime, and about twice the number for a dog in the full vigour of his strength. As a rule, dogs under eighteen months old are not likely to do themselves or their owners much good if bred from ; and availing one's self of the services of a very old dog is always risky. It is extremely hard to state an age at which a dog can be said to be " old " ; some retain the vigour of their youth up to ten years and more, whilst others get decrepit and break up at six or seven. So much depends upon constitution and careful attendance, that it is impossible to advise upon the age at which a stud dog ceases to be of use ; but breeders should see the dog for themselves, if they do not know him, and judge, from his appearance and condition, whether he is likely to suit their wishes.

On the arrival of a bitch for service, the owner of the stud dog should, unless time is a matter of consideration, fasten her up securely, and let her recover from the fatigues of her journey before the introduction takes place. A night's rest and a feed are very likely to assist nature's course, a bitch served immediately after a tiring journey being far more likely to miss conception than one who has rested and become a little accustomed to the place and those around her. Many bitches are very troublesome and restive when with the dog, and throw themselves about in a most violent manner; others are savage and morose, and if not carefully looked after are likely to fly at him and perhaps do some serious injury. In such cases the bitch must be held by the collar, but care should be taken that she does not get half suffocated by too tight a grasp being placed on it. The possibility of a fight taking place, or of the dog requiring some assistance, especially in the case of young bitches, make it undesirable that the pair should be left alone together for any length of time, much less after connection is terminated.

After union it is some time before the animals can be separated : twenty minutes is about the average, though, of course, this period is often exceeded or decreased in duration. After that the breeder must wait patiently for Nature to take its course, when the bitch should be kenneled by herself on straw, and kept as quiet as possible. It is desirable that a second visit should, if possible, be paid after an interval of thirty-six or forty-eight hours. The majority of the owners of stud dogs gladly consent to this arrangement, as it lessens the chances of the bitch proving barren, and also saves them trouble, and their dog from getting a bad name as a stock-getter.

A sire should be looked upon with suspicion if his services are in too great request, and the number of his receptions unlimited, as it is only reasonable to expect sickly offspring from a dog whose stud experiences are practically unrestricted. A very old dog, unless mated to a young and vigorous bitch, is more than likely to fail to beget stock at all: and if he succeeds in doing so, the puppies are very frequently of bad constitution and delicate in their earlier days. It is often the case that the services of a successful show dog are most eagerly sought after by breeders, and the merits of his *father* entirely overlooked; and this is certainly a fact which must puzzle all practical men when they reflect upon it. A sire of good pedigree, who can produce stock of superior quality to himself, is better worth patronising at a low fee than his successful son who has yet to prove himself the success at the stud which he is on the bench or in the field ; especially as in the latter instance the sum charged for his services is sure to be a considerable one. Many of our champion dogs have turned out complete failures from a breeder's point of view ; whilst their plainer-looking fathers or brothers have begotten offspring of a far better stamp, though with only half the chances of success. A golden rule in dog-breeding is, for the owner to satisfy himself that his bitch *really does* visit the dog he has selected for her. In many instances we know tricks to have been played upon owners who have sent their bitches to dogs at a distance ; and we have ourselves been applied to for the services of a dog, standing at a low fee, by an owner of a stud dog, for a bitch sent up to the latter. Unfortunately, in ignorance of the fact, we granted his request, and only afterwards discovered what had occurred, and that the bitch, the name of whose owner we never ascertained, had been sent up to this gentleman's dog, and was not one of his own. The difference between the fees of the two dogs was three guineas; and as it was impossible for us to *prove* that the owner was not informed of what took place, we were unable to take steps in the matter, and our acquaintance still walks the streets an honest man. If the distance is too far to accompany the bitch or send one's man, it is a very good plan to get a friend in the neighbourhood of the stud dog's kennel to accompany her when she visits him, especially in dealing with strangers. Of course, in the case of owners whose characters are above suspicion these precautions are unnecessary ; but it will always be a satisfaction to the proprietor of a stud dog to know that the bitch's visit has been witnessed by her owner or his nominee, especially if she should fail to be in pup. In event of the latter being the case, the usual practice is that the same bitch may visit the dog a second time gratuitously, or another of the same owner's at half price; but here again caution must be exercised on the part of the proprietor of the stud dog, for instances have occurred when puppies have been born dead, and he has been told there was no result from the union of the parents. Owners of stud dogs often do, and always should, provide the owners of bitches which have visited them with formal certificates of service; such documents are particularly useful in event of disputed pedigrees.

THE BROOD BITCH.

Young bitches often exhibit symptoms of an inclination to breed at the age of eight or nine months, but it is undesirable to place them at the stud until they have reached the age of at least eighteen months. The remarks we made above against the advisability of resorting to the services of too young a sire, apply with even greater force when a youthful bitch is under consideration. Stunted and puny puppies are almost sure to be produced from a young mother; and the injury they are likely to do her constitution is incalculable. It must be borne in mind that for weeks before birth her system is sorely taxed to provide them with nourishment, and after the shock of labour is gone through there is a further strain upon her until they are weaned.

The first symptom afforded by a bitch that she is likely to be soon ready for breeding purposes, is a desire on her part to romp and play with any dog she meets. This may possibly arise from merely exuberance of spirits, but it is always well to keep a close eye upon her as soon as any undue levity is observed in her conduct. It is most desirable to use every endeavour to keep the animal away from all risk of being got at by strange dogs; and when the matter is placed beyond doubt all former precautions should be doubled if possible. It must be remembered that there is not only a great risk of dogs getting into the place where the bitch is confined, but that she will probably be equally anxious to escape from her kennel, and some bitches have performed almost incredible feats in their endeavours to do so.

She should, if at a distance, be sent off to the kennels where the dog is standing a day or two after the earlier symptoms appear, so as to be in time. If despatched by public conveyance, it is imperative that she be securely confined in a box or basket from which escape is impossible. The transit of dogs has been more fully treated in the chapter on exhibiting, and need not be further alluded to here; but all breeders should be equally impressed with the absolute necessity of exercising the greatest vigilance when they have bitches by them under such circumstances. For at least a week after the bitch has visited the dog, the precautions for isolating her must not be relaxed, or all her owner's hopes may be marred by her forming a connection with a stranger.

The influence of a previous sire on a subsequent litter of puppies is a subject of the keenest discussion and interest amongst breeders, and a most interesting correspondence has taken place in the columns of the *Live Stock Journal* relating thereto. Some of the statements which have appeared from time to time in that journal upon this subject, and which have been substantiated by the names of writers whose position as breeders of various varieties of live stock is assured, are invested with a peculiar importance. But having carefully read and considered the matter, we find ourselves driven back on the supposition that although such occurrences undoubtedly have arisen, they are not by any means the matter-of-course events some of the correspondents of the *Live Stock Journal* consider them, and in more than one instance we have failed to satisfy ourselves that the influences imputed have regulated the course of events. In making this statement we attribute to the writers no desire to impose on public credulity, but we think they have too often forgotten the influence which surrounding objects exercise over the mind of a pregnant female. This opinion is shared by many breeders of live stock, and it is notorious that a celebrated breeder of black polled cattle had his premises and fences tarred, with the express object of assisting Nature in keeping the colour of his stock as deep as possible. It is, however, quite impossible for us to go at length into the subject, and it must therefore be dismissed with the remark that as many breeders firmly believe, from personal experience, that such a thing as past influence is possible, especially in the case of maiden bitches, due vigilance should be exercised in the thorough isolation of bitches when in season, or more than a temporary evil and disappointment may occur

PUPPING.

Having selected a proper mate for his bitch, and sent her to him, all anxiety is removed from an owner's mind for some time at least ; for during the first period of going with young, the bitch will require no special diet or attention. It may be here stated, for the benefit of the uninitiated, that the period of gestation amongst dogs is sixty-three days, and that this time is rarely exceeded unless something is wrong, though it sometimes occurs that the whelps make their appearance some days before they are expected. During this period the bitch should be allowed plenty of exercise, but during the latter portion of her pregnancy she is peculiarly liable to chills ; every care should therefore be taken to avoid any risk of her taking cold, and all washing operations and *violent* exercise must then be suspended. Our own experience has taught us that in the majority of instances it is almost impossible to tell whether or no the bitch is in whelp until the third or fourth week, and on many occasions we have known breeders to be in doubt for a much longer period ; in fact, on discussing with a very well-known Pointer exhibitor the accouchement of one of his exhibits during a show, he assured us that when she left home she had shown no traces of being in whelp, and as a matter of fact her time was not up until the following week.

A week or so before the date on which it is expected that she will whelp, the bitch should be installed in the quarters in which it is arranged the interesting event is to take place. The reason for this is that dogs must get used to a kennel before they will make themselves at home in it, and this feeling is peculiarly perceptible in the case of a bitch who has recently whelped ; for in many cases she will try and carry her puppies (greatly to the damage of the latter) back to her old quarters rather than let them remain in a kennel to which she is unaccustomed. Having got her reconciled to her change of abode, the *locale* of which should, if possible, be away from the other dogs, so as to let her have more quiet (but *warmth* and *absence of draught* are even more essential than isolation in such cases), and supposing the time of her whelping to be near at hand, it is desirable that the bitch should be provided with a diet of a more strengthening character than that which she has been in the habit of receiving. This need not consist entirely of meat or other heating foods, which can only tend to increase her discomfort in parturition, but may be made of scraps well boiled or stewed, with the addition of bread, meal, or rice, which in their turn will absorb the gravy or soup, and form, in conjunction with the scraps, when the latter are chopped up, a meal which is both wholesome and nutritious. A few days before the puppies make their appearance a considerable change is usually perceptible in the bitch ; the presence of milk can be detected, and a considerable enlargement of the stomach takes place. Her behaviour too, clearly indicates that she is uneasy and in pain, and in many instances the appetite entirely fails, and the bowels become confined. In the latter case a mild purgative of either castor, linseed, or sweet oil must be given. The first-named remedy is sometimes too powerful an aperient for a bitch in such a condition, as, in the more delicate breeds especially, it is apt to cause severe straining, which would injure the puppies. Before resorting, therefore, to castor-oil, an experimental dose of either linseed or sweet oil might be administered, which, if it succeed in acting on the bowels, will have satisfactorily accomplished the owner's object; and as the lubricating power of all three oils is essentially the same, the internal organs will be equally benefited by either medicine.

Two or three days before the puppies are due a good bed of straw should be provided, and this should not be changed till the whelps are at least a week old; for unnecessary attention will certainly worry the mother, and may cause her to destroy her offspring. The bed of straw should be placed on boards raised not higher than two or three inches from the ground; in fact, the bitch during the last few weeks of going in whelp should not be allowed the opportunity of leaping up and down on and off a high bench. On no account should the bed be placed on a cold stone or brick flooring; and even a carpet is objectionable, for the mother, in making her bed for the reception of her young, invariably removes all the bedding from underneath her, and piles it up at the sides in the shape of a nest. Her object in acting thus is to facilitate the operation of licking the puppies; as she will within a few hours of parturition have all her whelps thoroughly cleansed and freed from any offensive adherent matter, being during their earlier puppyhood most attentive to the personal cleanliness of her offspring. This would be impossible if she allowed them to lie on the straw, as the wet would soak into it and cause the bed to become foul.

The different temperaments and dispositions of various bitches become specially apparent as parturition approaches. Some will be impatient at the slightest intrusion on the solitude they evidently prefer, whilst others eagerly welcome the familiar voice of master or attendant, and seem to beg him to remain beside them in the time of suffering. A great deal must therefore be left to the judgment of those in charge of the bitch; but it should be borne in mind that, though an occasional visit is necessary even in the case of a most unsociably-disposed bitch, in order to see that nothing has gone wrong, still *too much* interference and fidgeting even with a quiet one is apt to render her feverish, and increase the difficulties of her situation. Under any circumstances a plentiful amount of cold water should always be placed near her, and beyond this she will, in the majority of instances, want nothing until the pups are born. Should she however become exhausted during labour, a little port wine may be given now and then. When safely delivered, some gruel should be given her, and she should be kept on this diet for the space of two or three days; it is strengthening and soothing to the internal organs, and can be made either with milk or water; the addition of a little gravy or beef tea is an excellent practice after the first two or three basins of gruel. The quantity of gruel should be unlimited, and very often she will devour a basinful every two or three hours for the first day; care, however, must be taken not to let it remain by her too long, so as to turn sour and disarrange the stomach, which it is very easy to do when a bitch has just whelped. It is always desirable to try and count the puppies when the mother is off the bed feeding, as it lets an owner know whether she eats her whelps or not; and if he misses puppies he must try and devise some way to stop the proceeding.

In event of a puppy dying, it must of course be removed at the first opportunity offering itself, and if this can be managed without the knowledge of the mother, so much the better; for we have known instances where a whole litter has been destroyed by a dam on the removal of one dead whelp from their midst; and, besides this, there is the danger of a bite from a bad-tempered bitch if she sees her family carried off. Opinions vary much as regards whether dogs can count or not; but our own belief is decidedly in favour of their being able to do so up to a certain number. This is a matter of considerable importance where puppies are concerned, for it is often necessary to remove some from the mother. Some bitches seem to take no notice of the diminished number of their family, whilst others appear frenzied by their bereavement, and, acting on a first impulse, have destroyed the remaining whelps, unless restrained from doing so. It being therefore certain that mothers are capable of discovering, by counting or otherwise, when any of their puppies have been removed in their absence, it behoves the breeder to be careful how he acts when such a course has to be adopted. If he carefully watches the bitch for half an hour or so on her re-introduction to her family, and sees that all is well, he need have no further care on that score; but should she become restless, and show signs of an inclination to destroy the remaining whelps, she must be closely guarded in order to prevent mischief. Some bitches are notorious for the habit they have of killing their puppies, and in such cases the only means to adopt is, in the absence of a foster-mother, to take the puppies in-doors, and keep them warmly wrapped up in a basket lined with flannel before a fire, and let the mother come and suckle them every two hours. Whilst with them she should be laid on her side, and gently held down so as to prevent her injuring them in any way.

Having alluded above to the subject of foster-mothers, we may express the opinion that, in the event of valuable puppies being expected, the acquisition of such an animal is very desirable. A bitch in whelp can often be obtained from the Dogs' Home, Battersea, for a few shillings, and if one is not to be obtained there in a suitable condition of pregnancy, Mr. Scorborio, the courteous and energetic manager of that institution can often put owners in the way of obtaining one at a very reasonable figure. Foster-mothers can also frequently be hired for a few weeks, if advertised for in the papers; and as a matter of fact we once obtained the services of seven at £1 each from one advertisement in the *Live Stock Journal.* The greatest precaution must however be exercised by owners, in order that no diseased or unhealthy bitch be received in the responsible position of wet-nurse to their puppies, for the danger of such an introduction can hardly be exaggerated; and therefore many persons rather shrink from investing in bitches of whose antecedents they are ignorant.

Aid from inexperienced persons when administered to a bitch in labour is almost sure to be attended with most unsatisfactory results, and we are simply re-echoing the opinion of the vast majority of practical breeders when we express the conviction that many of the so-called veterinary surgeons practising in this country know next to nothing of canine pathology. A man who may or may not have passed his examination at the Veterinary College, and professes to be an adept at physicking horses or doctoring cows, invariably considers himself quite qualified to attend upon dogs, and possibly in a few cases he may be so; but in most instances he knows less than the kennel-man does, and increases the ailing dog's difficulties by his injudicious treatment. "There is a man down the street who knows all about dogs," is a common saying when the owner is in a difficulty, and the man is sent for, generally turning out to be absolutely incompetent and grossly ignorant of what he professes to understand. For our own part we believe that doctoring their own dogs is an easy task for tolerably intelligent and fairly attentive owners, and experience has taught us that the list of drugs and remedies which are applicable to canine diseases is a very limited one indeed, and that an elaborate doggy pharmacopœia is a wholly unnecessary institution, which can only tend to complicate the difficulties which lie in the way of a beginner when he attempts to arrive at a correct diagnosis and treatment of his animal's ailments. In cases of protracted labour, where there are indications of internal complications, surgical aid must of course be rendered the bitch, provided really competent professional assistance can be obtained. All other is useless in such cases, and we must once again impress upon our readers the terrible danger and torture to which they subject their dogs by calling in the assistance of incompetent advisers. *Be convinced that your surgeon knows more than you do yourself,* is a golden rule for breeders to lay heed to.

In the event of the bitch being unable to pass her puppies after being in labour for some time, the application of crushed ice to the abdomen is frequently the means of enabling her to do so, as it has the effect of contracting the muscles of the womb, and thus assists in the expulsion of the whelps. Ergot is sometimes used in complicated cases as a uterine excitant, but should be resorted to only as an extreme measure, being, in the hands of inexperienced persons, a very dangerous medicine. Oiling the vagina is also in many cases a relief to the bitch. In some books we have seen it strongly recommended as a means of assisting protracted labour that the bitch should be immersed in a warm bath for a few minutes; this in ninety-nine cases out of a hundred involves two certain results—(1) almost instant relief to the dog, (2) DEATH. According to the theory propounded by Mayhew in his work on canine diseases, the application of warm water causes a relaxation of the muscles of the womb, whereas an exactly opposite effect is needed; thus the temporary relief from her suffering costs the poor beast her life, and her owner the mortification of having killed her by improper treatment. We know not of one only, but of scores of such instances occurring; and no doubt all breeders of experience are well acquainted with the ill effects of an injudicious bath to a bitch in labour.

Some curiosity on the part of a youthful breeder is natural enough where the first puppies of his own breeding are concerned; but he will be acting very foolishly indeed if he gives way to it. It cannot be any advantage to him to discover the sexes of the different whelps on the day of their birth, and all handling should be avoided unless it is thought desirable to remove some from the mother on account of the number being considered too many for her to bring up. It should be borne in mind that four or five strong, vigorous, well-nourished puppies are far more likely to turn out satisfactorily for their owner than eight or ten scantily-nourished ones; and it must be left to the good sense of the breeder to decide, from the condition of the bitch and the amount of milk she has secreted, how many she can do justice to without injuring herself. Five or six are enough for a moderate-sized bitch, and eight or ten for a large one. The extra ones can be destroyed if sickly, or placed under a foster-mother, if one can be got. In some instances puppies have been very successfully brought up by hand, through the immediate agency of a baby's feeding bottle; but before any one enters upon such an undertaking due consideration should be devoted to the magnitude of the task before him. Constant feeding is necessary, and the whelps require a great deal of warmth, patience, and attention. In circumstances like this the most valuable ally of all is to be found in the cook; if her hearty co-operation is obtained the chances are that the whelps will go on and prosper, for a snug corner for the basket on the kitchen hearth, and the constant supervision she can give them, is sure to benefit them very considerably.

About the ninth day the puppies begin to open their eyes, and very soon they commence crawling out of their nest and about the floor of the kennel; after which it is wonderful how fast they seem to grow and the strength they display. At two weeks old they will commence to eat bread-and-gravy, or bread-and-milk, if it is provided for them, though the latter is, we think, an objectionable diet, as it is apt to turn sour, and also, if cow's milk, to breed worms, to which young puppies are peculiarly liable. Goat's milk, however, we consider good for puppies, as it, according to our experience, does not increase the risk of worms. During this time the food given to the mother should be of a strengthening nature, so as to enable her to stand the strain on her constitution which her maternal duties involve, but care should be taken to prevent her bringing bones into her bed, as many instances have occurred of mothers severely biting their puppies who have attempted to take the bones from her. One or two gentle runs a day are now very necessary for the bitch, as exercise not only freshens her considerably, but gives her a chance of getting away from the persistent persecution which the puppies inflict upon her. At five weeks old the whelps may usually begin to be removed from their mother, and it is well to do this gradually, as they suffer less from the separation if this course is pursued; and by extending the intervals of the bitch's absence they can be almost entirely weaned without any ill effects to either themselves or their dam. The best method is to begin by removing the bitch for an hour or two in the warmest part of the day, so that the chance of the puppies catching cold is diminished. The periods of her absence can then be prolonged until she is only returned to them of a night, and finally ceases to visit them at all.

It frequently occurs that the teats of the bitch have been wounded by the teeth of the puppies when they suckle her; and inflammation, from the influx of milk, often arises when they are removed. Considerable relief can be obtained by rubbing some camphorated oil well over her stomach, and this can be repeated night and morning for some days, a mild dose of physic being administered when the puppies are finally removed. In the event, however, of the milk that she has secreted still bothering her, and her teats being so tender that drawing some off by ordinary milking is impossible recourse may be had to an ordinary soda-water bottle, heated with hot water, the mouth of which can be pressed over the inflamed teat. This has the effect of drawing some of the milk out, and thereby relieving the bitch of a great deal of pain. Or an ordinary breast-pump may be employed.

Having now given a brief sketch of the general treatment of a bitch when pupping, we will pass on to the future management of the whelps themselves.

REARING.

On the removal of the whelps from their mother, a very considerable change for the worse immediately takes place in their appearance, which is due mainly to the alteration in their diet and general mode of life. Instead of drawing a certain amount of sustenance from their dam at the cost of no trouble, they are now cast upon their own resources for a means of subsistence. The necessity of having to get up and hunt about for the dish which contains its food is a fact which it takes a puppy's mind a long time to master. Consequently the entire litter often passes many hungry hours during the night, although their food is within a few inches of their bed; and it is not until a happy thought strikes one of them that it might be a good plan if he got up and looked for something, that they all follow his example, and fall to as only hungry puppies can. Almost all puppies suffer greatly from worms, and immediately on their removal from their mother means should be taken to rid them of such torments. The presence of worms is certain when the stomachs of puppies swell and harden, but they frequently exist without developing such symptoms. It is therefore the safer plan to administer one or two doses of worm medicine all round, especial care being taken that their delicate mouths and throats are not injured in administering the remedy. The two best vermifuges are areca-nut and santonine. The latter, in its crystallised form, is an excellent remedy for worms in dogs, and about two grains in butter cannot be surpassed as a vermifuge for puppies of seven or eight weeks old, whose parents weigh from forty to sixty pounds weight. If too strong a dose is given, santonine has a tendency to affect the brain and cause fits, so precaution must be exercised in administering this medicine. The chief difficulty in the use of areca-nut lies in getting it freshly grated, as if allowed to become stale it loses its virtue as an anthelmintic. To avoid this the nut should be grated on an ordinary nutmeg-grater, and given immediately in butter or lard. The ordinary dose is two grains for every pound the dog weighs, but more than two drachms should never be given. Spratt's worm powders are also excellent remedies, if an owner has to clear his pets of these pests, and are easily procured of any chemist.

It is useless to resort to any remedy for worms in dogs unless the medicine is administered on an empty stomach. Small dogs should fast for at least twelve hours, and large powerful animals for twenty-four, before the medicine is administered. It is also desirable to prevent their drinking too much water during the period of their abstention, the object being to deprive the worms of all sorts of food, so that the anthelmintic may have a greater chance of success. Many persons give a dose of castor-oil the night before the vermifuge is given, and a second one two or three hours after if it has had no effect. As long as the purgative does not tax the dog's system too powerfully, these precautions materially assist the operation of the medicine; but judgment and caution must, of course, be exercised, and it would be foolish to adopt such vigorous treatment with a weakly puppy.

Crushed biscuits, oatmeal-porridge, and bread-and-gravy, with the addition of a little chopped meat and végetables, are the best diet for puppies when first away from their mother, and the amount they can get through in the course of twenty-four hours is considerable. The greatest care must be taken to guard against the puppies (this, in fact, applies to any dogs, but to puppies especially) being given food which is *sour or decomposed.* A very fruitful and common cause of this has only lately come to our knowledge. We are indebted for the following information to Mr. F. Gresham, whose experience in feeding large dogs is very considerable. This gentleman has proved by experience that food cooked in a copper or other boiler is very apt to turn sour as soon as cooked, if allowed to stand and cool *in the vessel in which it has been prepared.* Care should therefore be taken to remove it, as soon as the culinary operations are completed, to a cool and clean receptacle, where it can remain until it is required for the dogs, or is returned to the boiler, to be added to other meals in course of preparation.

All draughts should be kept away from their kennel, which must be warm and dry, or the puppies will not spread and grow as they should do; and a run in a dry yard is imperative, if the weather is not too cold or damp. By keeping his puppies clean and dry, an owner considerably lessens the risk of distemper ravaging his kennels, for this fearful scourge is unquestionably amenable to sanitary arrangements, and except on very rare occasions, when its origin can usually be traced, is scarcely ever present in well-conducted establishments. In our own kennels we have never experienced a single case of distemper amongst puppies of our own breeding, and this has been under circumstances of great difficulty, where for over three years an average of nearly fifty dogs have been kept in confined spaces. A strict attention to cleanliness, fresh air, fresh water, sound food, combined with proper grooming and exercise, renders the presence of distemper well-nigh impossible, and if a breeder who attends to these matters has the misfortune to have it communicated to his stock (for distemper *is* contagious), he will find them the better able to resist its attacks if they have been previously well looked after.

Our own treatment in the few cases we had in cases of puppies we had bought (one or two of which sickened within the week) were thorough and absolute isolation in the first place, so as to preclude all possibility of contagion or infection in case of other diseases. We had a lumber-room attached to the house cleared for a hospital, and fitted with a gas stove; by this means a steady even temperature can be maintained night and day, and this is a most important feature in the treatment of distemper. All stuffiness in the air should be avoided, for it must be remembered that in this disease the nostrils become charged with a thick fluid which renders breathing very difficult. We invariably had the window open at the top, and with the gas stove aided by a thermometer kept the room at a steady temperature of 60 degrees. The only food given was beef-tea with some bread soaked in it, and the only medicine Rackham's distemper pills. Seeing is believing, and we believe these pills to be almost infallible in the treatment of distemper, never having lost a dog when using them, and knowing many breeders who share our opinion, we cannot resist alluding to them. When the graver symptoms begin to subside solid food can be administered, and the dog picks up wonderfully soon, though too premature an introduction to the cold outside is to be deprecated after his confinement so long in a warm temperature. A friend—we rather think it was Mr. R. Fulton, of Brockley—once told us of a food which he considered a capital change for dogs suffering from distemper, and this was a number of fresh haddocks' heads put into a pot and covered with water, to be boiled until the bones of the fish get soft and the water is almost entirely absorbed; this, when cold, forms a jelly, which is keenly appreciated by the invalids, and seems to do them good. Our friend's theory was that the phosphorus contained in the fish-bones assisted the medicine in curing the dog; but be this as it may, it is certain that no ill effects, but rather the contrary, resulted from giving it them.

Allusion having thus been made to the two greatest plagues of puppyhood—worms and distemper—there hardly remain more diseases to which they are peculiarly liable. Fits they certainly often suffer from, but these almost invariably are the result of worms, and will subside and disappear when the irritating cause of their presence is removed. Teething occasionally troubles them, but seldom to any great extent, for puppies do not usually shed their first teeth until nine months old, and then they are strong enough to bear the pain and annoyance of the cutting of their new ones inflicts upon them. Should the puppies, however, appear to suffer from the swelling of their gums previous to the appearance of a tooth, it is well to lance the inflamed part, especially if the gum appears abnormally hard. Not only does this give immediate relief, but it helps the teeth to come up in a regular line, which in most varieties is most desirable.

The exercise and subsequent treatment of the whelps have been so thoroughly gone into in the chapters on general management and exercise, that no further allusion to them is requisite here.

LACTOL

— FOR —

Weaning and Rearing
Puppies and Kittens.

**NO COOKING REQUIRED—JUST ADD HOT WATER.
HUNDREDS OF UNSOLICITED TESTIMONIALS RECEIVED.
USED IN ALL THE LEADING KENNELS.**

THE most critical stage of a puppy's existence is the weaning period—from five to eight weeks old—when he is taken from the dam. Until the introduction of Lactol, puppies, as a general rule, were weaned on unsuitable foods, most unlike the mother's milk that they have but shortly left, with the result that they invariably suffered from indigestion, diarrhœa, vomiting, distended stomach, &c., and in many cases died.

An analysis of the milk of a bitch shows immediately why this should be the case, as it is seen to be three times as strong as cow's or goat's milk. The only food on which puppies can be safely weaned and reared is Lactol, which, when mixed with hot water as directed, forms a food three times as strong as cow's milk, and identical in taste, analysis, and appearance with the puppy's natural food.

It is regularly used and recommended by all the leading dog fanciers and canine specialists, and is most highly spoken of by the veterinary and kennel press.

In Tins, I/-, 2/6, 5/- and 20/-.

Of BOOTS', TAYLOR'S DRUG CO., WHITELEY'S, HARRODS, ARMY & NAVY STORES, and other leading Stores and Chemists, or from the Manufacturers :—

A. F. SHERLEY & CO., 46 & 48, BOROUGH HIGH ST., S.E.

b

The Kennel Library.

BRITISH DOGS.

Their Points, Selection, and Show Preparation. Third Edition. By eminent specialists. Beautifully Illustrated. This is the fullest work on the various breeds of dogs kept in England. In one volume, *demy 8vo, cloth, price 12/6 nett, by post 13/-.*

PRACTICAL KENNEL MANAGE-MENT.

A Complete Treatise on the Proper Management of Dogs, for the Show Bench, the Field, or as Companions, with a chapter on Diseases—their Causes and Treatment. By well-known Specialists. Illustrated. *In cloth, price 10/6 nett, by post 11/-.*

DISEASES OF DOGS.

Their Causes, Symptoms, and Treatment; Modes of Administering Medicines; Treatment in cases of Poisoning, &c. For the use of Amateurs. By HUGH DALZIEL. Fourth Edition. Entirely Re-written and brought up to date. By ALEX. C. PIESSE, M.R.C.V.S. *Price 1/- nett, by post 1/2 ; in cloth, price 2/- nett, by post 2/3.*

BREAKING AND TRAINING DOGS.

Being Concise Directions for the proper education of Dogs, both for the Field and for Companions. Second Edition. By "PATHFINDER." Many new Illustrations. *In cloth, price 6/6 nett, by post 6/10.*

POPULAR DOG KEEPING:

Being a Handy Guide to the General Management and Training of all Kinds of Dogs for Companions and Pets. Third Edition. By J. MAXTEE. Illustrated. *Price 1/- nett, by post 1/2.*

THE FOX TERRIER.

Its Points, Breeding, Rearing, Preparing for Exhibition. Second Edition, Revised and brought up to date. Fully Illustrated. *Price 1/- nett, by post 1/2.*

THE COLLIE,

As a Show Dog, Companion, and Worker. Revised by J. MAXTEE. Third Edition. Illustrated. *Price 1/- nett, by post 1/2.*

THE GREYHOUND :

Its Points, Breeding, Rearing, Training, and Running. Second Edition, Revised and brought up to date by J. MAXTEE, assisted by T. B. RIXON. Illustrated. *Price 1/- nett, by post 1/2.*

THE WHIPPET OR RACE-DOG.

How to Breed, Rear, Train, Race, and Exhibit the Whippet, the Management of Race Meetings, and Original Plans of Courses. By FREEMAN LLOYD. Illustrated. *Price 1/- nett, by post 1/2.*

BREEDERS' AND EXHIBITORS' RECORD,

For the Registration of Particulars concerning Pedigree Stock of every Description. By W. K. TAUNTON. In three parts. *In cloth, price each 2/6 nett, or the set 6/- nett, by post 6/6.*

Part I., The Pedigree Record.   Part II., The Stud Record.
Part III., The Show Record.

Kennel Indispensables.

The Ideal Disinfectant

Famous as a cure for Mange, Eczema, Ringworm, and all other parasitic skin diseases.

A GRAND HAIR PRODUCER.

Destroys all insects such as fleas, lice, ticks, etc.

Sold in tins at 9d., 1|3, 2|- each; 6|- per gallon.
Free for P.O.

The Kennel, the Stable, the Poultry Yard kept sweet and healthy.
Ask for IZAL Veterinary Pamphlet.

IZAL Disinfectant Powder.

THE STRONGEST POWDER KNOWN.

In tins, 6d. and 1|- each; 50 lb. casks, 5|-. Free for P.O.

IZAL Soft Soap, 8d. per lb. Post free.
IZAL Bar Soap. 8d. per lb. Post free.

Special quotations for large lots.

NEWTON, CHAMBERS & Co., Ltd.,
THORNCLIFFE, NEAR SHEFFIELD.

BARNARDS LIMITED, NORWICH

IMPROVED RANGE OF KENNELS AND RUNS.
No. 347.

Each kennel, 6ft. wide, 5ft. deep. Runs, each 6ft. long, 6ft. wide, finished in the very best style.

One House and Run	**£7 10**	**0**	
Two Houses and Runs	**12 15**	**0**	
Three ditto	**18 18**	**0**	
Six ditto	**35 0**	**0**	
Carriage Paid.			

NEW PORTABLE KENNEL AND RUN.
Registered Design.
No. 345.

3ft. 6in. wide, 8ft. long, 4ft. high	**£4 5**	**0**	
4ft. wide, 9ft. 6in. long, 5ft. high	**5 10**	**0**	
5ft. wide, 12ft. long, 5ft. high	**7 10**	**0**	
Carriage Paid.			

IMPROVED KENNEL.
No. 348.

AWARDED GOLD MEDAL SCHEVENINGEN,
1901 and 1906.

For Terriers ...	**£1 7**	**6**	
For Collies, &c.	**2 5**	**6**	
For Mastiffs ...	**3 9**	**6**	
Carriage Paid.			

LEAN-TO PORTABLE KENNEL AND RUN.
No. 346

House, 4ft. by 3ft. 6in. Run, 4ft. by 6ft.

Cash Price	**£5 0**	**0**	
Wood Back for Run,	**22/6** extra.		
Corrugated Iron round Run	**5/-** extra.		
Reversible Trough	**5/-**		
Carriage Paid.			

CATALOGUE FREE:
Norfolk Iron Works, Norwich.

CPSIA information can be obtained at www.ICGtesting.com
Printed in the USA
LVOW06s1733030115

421357LV00001B/113/P